LIFE'S LIVING TOWARD DYING

Life's Living toward Dying

~

A Theological and Medical-Ethical Study

VIGEN GUROIAN

WILLIAM B. EERDMANS PUBLISHING COMPANY
GRAND RAPIDS, MICHIGAN / CAMBRIDGE, U.K.

© 1996 Wm. B. Eerdmans Publishing Co.
255 Jefferson Ave. S.E., Grand Rapids, Michigan 49503 /
P.O. Box 163, Cambridge CB3 9PU U.K.

Printed in the United States of America

01 00 99 98 97 96   7 6 5 4 3 2 1

ISBN 0-8028-4190-2

Portions of Chapter 4 appeared in slightly different form in the author's book *Ethics after Christendom: Toward an Ecclesial Christian Ethic* (Grand Rapids: William B. Eerdmans, 1994), pp. 176-83.

Unless otherwise noted, the Scripture quotations in this publication are from the New Revised Standard Version of the Bible, copyright © 1989 by the Division of Christian Education of the National Council of Churches of Christ in the U.S.A., and used by permission.

To

F. Richard Vranian

(1921-1992)

As for me, I am already being poured out as a libation, and the time of my departure has come. I have fought the good fight, I have finished the race, I have kept the faith. From now on there is reserved for me the crown of righteousness, which the Lord, the righteous judge, will give me on that day, and not only to me but also to all who have longed for his appearing.

2 Timothy 4:6-8

Contents

Acknowledgments

WE STOOD together at the bottom of the cavernous Hyatt atrium in Atlanta, Georgia, in the fall of 1987. It was the last annual meeting of the American Academy of Religion that Paul Ramsey would attend. In a year and several months, his looming presence would be with us no longer. He was complaining of his throat and regularly made attempts to clear it. He did not know as yet that this was not an ordinary bout with old esophagus problems, that this time it was cancer.

Over the previous several years, Paul Ramsey had taken note of the work I was doing in Orthodox ethics. Indeed, he had already reviewed the proofs of my first book, *Incarnate Love: Essays in Orthodox Ethics,* and written some very kind words for the back cover. During his many years as a preeminent voice in Christian ethics, he had encouraged the youngsters who were coming up. Now it was my turn, and I was profoundly grateful.

But Paul was always pushing you to go on and do other things. "You know," I said to him, "I think the Orthodox rites of burial might be the richest sources of the theology of the church." "Then you must do something with them," he said. I paused. Yes, that was an idea. I thought perhaps something on the theology of death and

ix

especially the practical dimensions of caring for the dying. Little did I know that Paul Ramsey, who had written so much himself on these subjects, would be attending to his own dying over the next year. I promised him as we parted that I would take him up on his challenge.

Four years later, I wrote an essay entitled "Death and Dying Well in the Orthodox Liturgical Tradition." Martin Marty read it on a plane and asked me to submit it to *Second Opinion,* where it was subsequently published. In a footnote I expressed my indebtedness to Paul Ramsey for having encouraged me in the undertaking. A revised version of this essay became the last chapter of my book *Ethics after Christendom: Toward an Ecclesial Christian Ethic* (1994). I thought of Paul Ramsey often as I wrote the entire book, and I miss him still.

Others have encouraged me along the way as well. William F. May was at the conference in 1991 at which I read the original essay. At the time, he suggested that I might have the beginnings of a book and offered some suggestions that later helped me to sort out just what shape I wanted to give the final product. Gilbert Meilaender and Allen Verhey read an early draft and wrote lengthy and very helpful critiques. Later, due to the latter's suggestion, I was invited to deliver several lectures at the Institute of Religion at the Baylor College of Medicine in Houston. These lectures evolved into the preface and final chapter of the book. Prof. James Childress, whom I have known, as his student and colleague, for more than twenty-five years, encouraged me from the start, even in the midst of personal tragedy, when he lost his wife, Georgia, to an incurable illness. Over the years, Nathan A. Scott Jr. has continuously encouraged me to reach into the liturgical tradition of Orthodox Christianity for theological and moral reflection, as I have done in this study.

Among Orthodox theological colleagues, Fr. Stanley Harakas and Fr. John Breck lent support. Over the past five years, they have graciously joined me in several forums on medical ethics sponsored by the Prelacy of the Armenian Church of America under the inspiration of His Eminence Archbishop Mesrob Ashjian. I must also give special thanks to Sharon M. Burns, RSM, who was my chair at Loyola College in the early 1980s and then went on to serve as a chaplain at Stella Maris Hospice in Towson, Maryland, where she currently serves. Conversations I had with her in the spring of 1993 helped to shape the final chapter of the book in significant ways.

In 1993, the Earhart Foundation awarded me a grant that permitted a semester's leave. I am extremely grateful for that support, without which I do not think the book would have gotten written. I remain in debt to the late Russell Kirk and his wife, Annette, for taking a special interest in this project and for supporting my application for the Earhart Foundation grant.

Dr. Carol Nevin Abromaitis of the English department at Loyola College read an early draft of the manuscript and put her fine editing skills to work with good results. Elizabeth Obara, a brave undergraduate student at Loyola College, took up a call for assistance issued in my Honors Ethics Seminar and helped with the indexing. In my four years of association with Eerdmans, I have grown to appreciate and respect the conviction and vision that editor-in-chief Jon Pott brings to his profession, and I want to thank him personally for his keen editorial eye and willingness to push me, sometimes against my own inertia, toward a higher standard of writing. I owe a very special word of thanks to my editor T. A. Straayer at Eerdmans. He has made the final product a much better book than it would have been otherwise.

In August of 1992, my father-in-law, F. Richard Vranian, succumbed to liver cancer after a long struggle. Dick did not realize how much he was teaching me along the way. He died well, to the end a good husband of his wife, Flora; father of my wife, June; grandfather of my children, Rafi and Victoria; and a gentleman always. I loved him as a second father and as a friend, and I have dedicated this book to his memory.

Dr. Kevorkian and the
Thanatos Syndrome

THE TRUTH about life and death and about living and dying that the Christian church has proclaimed for millennia is being severely tested in our day. Perhaps no recent public figure is more representative of this monumental shift in morality than Dr. Jack Kevorkian. His crusade to legalize physician-assisted suicide (or euthanasia) is more than an effort to press the logic of "freedom of choice" one step further. It is an attack on the fundamental presuppositions of the Judeo-Christian tradition and the moral limits it sets on the giving and taking of life. Thus, it seems appropriate to begin this book on the theological meaning of death and a Christian ethics of caring for the dying with a discussion of the challenge presented by Kevorkian and the euthanasia movement.

In his last novel, *The Thanatos Syndrome,* the late Southern writer Walker Percy offers us a picture of an America in which Kevorkian's dreams have been realized, in which the U.S. Supreme Court has ruled that people have a right not to have to "suffer a life of suffering," that they have a right to be put to death with dignity. To ensure these rights, the federal government runs "Qualitarian centers" that practice the sort of medicine that Kevorkian advocates, offering abortion and euthanasia as routine therapies for the physically and mentally impaired, the "unwanted" and socially "useless." In this fictional American society, the capacity to rationalize killing, from fetuses to those in geriatric wards, knows no limit. Americans have invented for themselves the right to inflict death on others as they would have others inflict death on them.

A principal character in the story is an eccentric priest, Fr. Simon Smith, who is finding it difficult to live out his vocation in the midst of this moral chaos. He serves a flock of successful, respectable modern narcissists, some of whom view him as a failed priest because he refuses to provide them with the sort of divine therapy they are looking for. But there is more to his "failure" than meets the eye.

As the story begins, Fr. Smith has fled his responsibilities in a hospice and climbed to the top of a fire tower, where he is praying and meditating. In doing so, however, he has not turned his face from the evils being committed around him — especially the false care for the dying that is being provided in the government Qualitarian centers. Nor does he withdraw judgment from the lives of people who want to believe that there is no such thing as final accountability for one's life, that all we need expect of ourselves is to be well adjusted, tolerant of others, and "decent" toward our fellow human beings, even — in fact, especially — when putting them to death. He is simply frustrated by the fact that the value which the church has traditionally placed on life is no longer much evident among his parishioners.

Looking out over those parishioners as he preaches a sermon at the close of the novel, Fr. Smith is halted by their complacency and their inability to comprehend their complicity in the evil surrounding them. "I don't see any sinners here," he says. "Everyone looks justified. No guilt here! . . . Not a guilty face here."[1] These wry words belie the reason Fr. Smith climbed the fire tower in the

1. Percy, *The Thanatos Syndrome* (New York: Farrar, Straus & Giroux, 1987), pp. 360-61.

first place. At least one of his parishioners sees through the irony, however: "For God's sake. Like Jonah, I mean, really. Has it ever occurred to anybody that he might be up there for a much simpler, more obvious reason? . . . He could be doing vicarious penance for the awful state of the world."[2]

His parishioners view Fr. Smith as anything from a hopeless eccentric to a dangerous lunatic. Yet Percy manages to make his beliefs thoroughly consistent with the traditional Christian understanding of human existence and the moral limits which that understanding places on the taking of human life. A Roman Catholic, Percy strongly suspected that once faith had been set aside, the limits to taking human life that had traditionally belonged to the Western ethos would not be able to stand up against the pressure to legalize physician-assisted suicide and the whole drift of the thanatos syndrome. He certainly believed that the cultural crisis associated with the thanatos syndrome is also a crisis within American Christianity. The church as a whole was failing to talk straight about death, and Percy was convinced that this failure was rooted in language itself. "So decrepit and so abused is the language of the Judeo-Christian religions that it takes an effort to salvage them, the very words, from the husks and barnacles of" false meaning.[3]

The media may initially have given Kevorkian the title "Dr. Death" in order to label him as an extreme and dangerous man. But Kevorkian himself has embraced the label, because death is in fact the passion of his life. He has assumed the role of high priest to our real-world thanatos syndrome. He is content to leave it to others to haggle over the meaning of life and when it begins and ends; his special interest is the dying process itself, the source of so much fear and obsession in the modern psyche. In his own peculiar

---

2. Percy, *The Thanatos Syndrome*, pp. 112-13.

3. Percy, "Why Are You a Catholic?" in *Signposts in a Strange Land* (New York: Farrar, Straus & Giroux, 1991), p. 306.

manner, Kevorkian has grasped a truth that his opponents do not understand: there will be no final word on the meaning of life without an equally final word on death. While the churches remain silent concerning the meaning of death, Kevorkian and others like him who misrepresent the nature of death can utter its name authoritatively and seek the power to administer it to people who are fearful of sickness and suffering.

In the midst of this crisis and confusion over the meaning of death, a figure like Dr. Kevorkian was bound to come along. It is not surprising that Kevorkian is a physician: people in our culture have come to view physicians as their chief mediators between life and death — a role that traditional societies reserved for the shaman or priest. Americans don't really believe that doctors possess the power to defeat death, but they do believe that doctors have a greater power than anyone else in our society to manipulate death, either to forestall it or to hasten it, and so it is to doctors that people turn for help to die when they have decided that the prospect of continuing to live is "unbearable."

In the winter of 1993, the *Baltimore Sun* ran a feature story entitled "Kevorkian Ally Calls Death a Lifestyle." At the time, Kevorkian was conducting a hunger strike in a Michigan jail where he was being held on charges that he had violated the state's law against assisting an individual to commit suicide. The article was about John B. Tydings, a man from Maryland who, together with others, was offering to post $50,000 in bail for Kevorkian. Tydings threatened to kill himself if Kevorkian died during his hunger strike. He "just didn't want to live in a world where Dr. Kevorkian was not alive to fight for the right to die."[4] In the end, Kevorkian was set free after promising a judge that he "would not help anyone else die while an appeals court considers the constitutionality of assisted

4. Jay Apperson, "Kevorkian Ally Calls Death a Lifestyle," *Baltimore Sun*, 19 December 1993, p. 1B.

suicide." But for Tydings, the issues were larger. He rejected " 'an-tiquated' attitudes toward death" and claimed to have invented his own religion in which death with all its residual sacral power is a god. He went on to say,

> We tend to look upon death as the ultimate evil, when in reality it is the ultimate *solution*. . . . Life is not always good, and death is not always bad. . . . It's my thesis that only by embracing death emotionally as well as intellectually can we get the firmest possible grip on life. So I consider myself as much pro-life as pro-death.[5]

Eccentric? Crazy? I don't think so. In promoting his own thanatos religion, Tydings is representative of increasing numbers of people in our society who are trying to piece together new strategies for dealing with death in a postmodern environment no longer perva-sively informed by the life-affirming principles of biblical faith.

Kevorkian speaks as a prophet of what he calls "medicide" and "obitiatry." In his book *Prescription Medicide: The Goodness of Planned Death,* Kevorkian presents his case in clear terms. While he badly misrepresents biblical faith, he accurately assesses the contem-porary crisis of faith and ethics. He writes of an "ethical vacuum" created in our society by the demise of the old morality to which the medical profession had subscribed. The "inflexible and harshly punitive Judeo-Christian dogma that espoused the absolute and inviolable 'sanctity' of human life" no longer dominates the culture, says Kevorkian.[6] Everything is in flux, and medicine reflects this crisis.

Kevorkian argues that until recently theistic superstitions and

---

5. Tydings, quoted by Apperson in "Kevorkian Ally Calls Death a Lifestyle," p. 2B; italics mine.

6. Kevorkian, *Prescription Medicide: The Goodness of Planned Death* (Buffalo, N.Y.: Prometheus Books, 1991), p. 240. Subsequent references to this volume will be made parenthetically in the text.

sacral taboos inhibited genuine human autonomy and prevented the acceptance of a pragmatic situation ethics. But he is confident that the future of medicine will not resemble the past. Physicians once embraced a uniform medical code, but in the future they will have no need for such a code, he predicts, because they will be obliged to respect the individual's autonomy as the highest value. "Under . . . conditions of patients' autonomy coupled with medical competence and honesty, how could any overwhelming or insuperable bioethical problem arise?" he asks rhetorically. "And would an official bioethical code be at all necessary? Or even useful?" (p. 175).

Kevorkian sees himself as the pioneer of a new breed of physicians who, freed of any lingering taint of the old absolutism and paternalism, unhesitatingly affirm individual autonomy as the highest value. "If a patient's personal creed forbids a medically indicated blood transfusion, for example, then a truly ethical doctor would not give it and would not dispute the patient's decision to refuse it," says Kevorkian. "In fact, the doctor would be obligated to protest any kind of legal or judicial interference" (pp. 175-76). Kevorkian has mastered the language of a post-Christian therapeutic and individualistic culture. He has seen accurately enough that, in a society that embraces autonomy as the highest good, the "right to die" cannot be denied much longer. He points out that we have already modified our law to overturn the old theism's absolute prohibitions against suicide and abortion. He judges that "no matter what legal or religious injunctions are imposed in the foreseeable future, these two taboos will never again withstand the evolving pressures of contrary demand" (p. 240). He confidently predicts that the stigma attached to euthanasia will be the next to fall. In November of 1994, Oregon voters narrowly passed Measure 16, making it legal for physicians to prescribe lethal drugs for patients who have been diagnosed as having six months or less to live, lending further credence to Kevorkian's predictions. Other states are bound to follow.

Kevorkian confidently maintains that in the future medicine will be truly therapeutic and thus finally live up to its ancient potential: it will displace Judeo-Christian religion as the mediator between life and death. In fact, Kevorkian ironically echoes St. Paul's promise in 1 Corinthians 15 that in the future death will lose its sting — though in Kevorkian's version this will come to pass not because of what God does but because a medicine that has come of age will tame and lend new meaning to death by using it as a therapy for unwanted and unbearable suffering. Medicine may not yet be able to master death completely, but it is on the way to securing the power to manipulate it therapeutically in order to relieve people of the fear that chronic or terminal illness might one day make their lives desolate and meaningless without relief.

At the close of his book, Kevorkian exhorts the medical profession and society at large to boldly take the next step toward a new age of *medicide* — his term for the practice of euthanasia in an institutional setting with the assistance of professional medical personnel (doctors, nurses, paramedics, physician's assistants, medical technologists). He also advocates *obitiatry* — routine experimentation on the dying and the dead in this context in order to enlarge our understanding of the death process. "The time has come," he says, "to let medicide extend a comforting hand to those slipping into the valley of death, and to let obitiatry extract from their ebbing vitality the power to illuminate some of its darkest recesses for those who come after them" (p. 203).

Kevorkian insists that "medicine and religion should be *completely* divorced from one another" (p. 170). But in fact the sort of medicine he is promoting is not an alternative to religion but rather a new kind of religion. He even invests it with a kind of redemptive power — a dark parallel to the redemptive power of Christ — and he worships man rather than God as the lord of life. He ends his book with this exhortation:

The time has come to smash the last irrational and most fearsome taboo of planned death and thereby to open the floodgates of equally momentous benefit for humankind. In the first place, . . . the positive euthanasia of obitiatry would expand enormously the amplitude and intensity of the ordinary "visible spectrum." It would do this by allowing doctors for the first time to carry out on living human beings otherwise impossible trials of new and untested drugs, devices, or operations. That would accelerate medical progress by eliminating the need for experiments on animals or ill patients who volunteer to be test subjects. But the biggest impact of obitiatry will probably be its extension of the abstract spectrum of medicine into the opposite "invisible in-fradeath" realm, where the real potential for serious investigation of the phenomenon of death is to be found. (P. 241)

What shall we make of all this? As I see it, Kevorkian's views have grown out of a corruption of two truths of biblical faith concerning God and human existence — a corruption that has become regrettably common in contemporary society. Christians have traditionally maintained (1) that the death of human beings is a great evil precisely because it negates God's gift of life to the creature whom he created in his own image and likeness and for whom God intended immortality, and (2) that God risked the possibility of death when he gave human beings a free will and relative autonomy. There is obviously a certain amount of natural tension between these truths, but biblical faith holds them in relationship, allowing each to balance and qualify the other. As our society has abandoned the authority of biblical faith, it has tended to dissolve the antinomic relationship between the two truths, remove them from their appropriate biblical and theological contexts, and elevate each truth separately to the status of absolute axiomatic principle. One party sees death as the greatest evil (the *summum malum*) and contends that life is a "sacred" absolute that must be preserved at all costs and must not be taken by human hands under any circumstances. A second party champions human autonomy and "freedom of choice," including the prerogative to end life when suffering is unbearable or when it lacks "quality." As William F. May has observed, both parties "revere a creaturely good, not the Creator."[7]

Into the dark confusion of the cultural eclipse of biblical faith steps Dr. Jack Kevorkian. This is not to say that he fits easily within either cultural party, pro-life or pro-choice. To be sure, Kevorkian is a champion of human autonomy, but he calls the bluff of the advocates of "freedom of choice" by pressing their claims toward conclusions that they themselves assiduously avoid. He consciously steps beyond the ethics of freedom of choice by outright rejecting religious definitions of life and death as well as the limits on taking life respected by the old humanism. His new science of obitiatric medicine, liberated from traditional restraints, is aimed at exploring the outmost reaches (or limitless horizons) of human autonomy. In *Prescription Medicide,* Kevorkian writes,

> The fear of being seen as killers intimidates doctors. Some mistakenly try to equate with murder the act of executing a peacetime death sentence. But how can that be? The law defines murder as "criminal homicide . . . committed with malice aforethought . . . , and committed recklessly under circumstances manifesting extreme indifference to the value of human life." It is obvious that this cannot apply to a doctor who has been permitted to experiment on, or to take organs from, a willing criminal being executed. In fact, the doctor's act would manifest the highest regard for the value of human life in the most emphatic sense.
>
> Yet, even when convinced that it's not murder, most doctors still object. What they fail to appreciate is that neither killing nor

---

7. May, *The Physician's Covenant: Images of the Healer in Medical Ethics* (Philadelphia: Westminster Press, 1983), p. 69.

homicide per se entails or implies criminal or unethical conduct.
(Pp. 162-63)

Kevorkian is disturbingly reminiscent of the suicide Kirilov in
Dostoevsky's novel *The Possessed.* Kirilov is committed to killing
himself not because he does not value his own life but because he puts
an even greater value on human freedom and autonomy. He is
convinced that God is a human invention and that there is no such
thing as life after death. So long as people believe in God and life after
death, they will continue to fall victim to the great "swindle" by
accepting without question the belief that "life is pain, life is fear."
Kirilov decides that it remains for one courageous man to expose the
swindle and make the way for the "real man." It is necessary that one
man kill himself in order to kill the fear of death itself, to show that
death is not the limit of human freedom but the key to its complete
realization. "One day there will be free, proud men to whom it will
make no difference whether they live or not. That'll be the new man.
He who conquers pain and fear will be god himself. And the other
God will disappear."[8] Kirilov accepts the burden of the task himself,
determining that he will commit suicide.

> To recognize that there's no God without recognizing at the same
> time that you yourself have become God makes no sense, for if
> it did, you'd have to kill yourself. . . . It is my duty to make myself
> believe that I do not believe in God. I'll be the first and the last
> to open the door. . . . For three years I've searched for the attribute
> of my divinity and I've found it — my freewill! This is all I have
> at my disposal to show my independence and the terrifying new
> freedom I have gained.[9]

8. Dostoevsky, *The Possessed,* trans. Andrew R. MacAndrew (New York: New
American Library, 1962), p. 111.
9. Dostoevsky, *The Possessed,* p. 637.

Kevorkian has devoted himself to a similar mission: he seeks to liberate doctors and dying patients from traditional religious and moral constraints. He will seize the right to help others commit suicide, he says, in order to relieve people of their suffering. But, like Kirilov, he has a larger agenda. He is trying to open the door to complete autonomy and freedom for the rest of humanity. In this he is going beyond the conscious aim of most people in the euthanasia movement. As William F. May has noted, "The euthanasia movement encourages engineering death rather than facing death. Euthanasia would bypass dying to get one dead as quickly as possible." The first impulse is to relieve suffering, not to kill. To some extent this strategy is an understandable response "to the quandaries of an age that makes dying such an inhumanly endless business," says May, and yet it is ironic that the movement "opposes the horrors of a purely technical death by using technique to eliminate the victim."[10]

Kevorkian wants to kill people not merely to relieve their suffering but also to usher in a new age of liberated science. Insofar as that is the case, he does not accurately represent the euthanasia movement as May describes it — but I suspect that he is nonetheless the prophet of its real future. Long before Kevorkian arrived on the scene, Paul Ramsey speculated about where the movement was headed. "The humanity of mankind is at stake in how . . . we go about assaulting the last taboo: death," he wrote.[11] He compared the euthanasia movement to the movement to liberate sex in the 1960s, warning that if the euthanasia movement were successful, the consequences would be far more revolutionary.

It is not simply that we hoped to improve matters in the first instance by chatting about sex all day long . . . , and now propose

10. May, *The Physician's Covenant,* p. 84.
11. Paul Ramsey, "Death's Pedagogy," in *Death, Dying, and Euthanasia* (Frederick, Md.: University Publications of America, 1980), p. 342.

to do the same about death. That policy was foredoomed to failure, and foreseeably so without a sound understanding of the *human* that can be either enhanced or violated by at least some opinions or actions in the realm of sexuality. Still largely without that normative guide to action and for social approval, we now have "calisthenic sexuality." . . .

The same outlook and program addressed to "the last taboo" can only lead eventually and logically to the same thing: to "calisthenic dying," i.e. deliberate death, administered death; and submission to the power of a widespread chatter that tells us again and again fables about "death with dignity." . . . That indeed spells the end of "intensive *care*" for the dying! . . . Can human beings be utterly desensitized and then reconstructed in their attitudes toward death — at least operationally toward the deaths of the useless — according to the requirements of instrumental social rationalism? It remains to be seen whether trepidation, awe and respect in the face of encounters with death because of the unique human beings therein made manifest, can withstand dissolution in this civilization any more than sexual relations between human embodied persons withstood reduction to "sturgeon for dinner."[12]

Ramsey argued that unless Christians formulate a contemporary ethic of death and dying with a compelling vision of human values and ends, pragmatism, utilitarianism, sensationalism, and a pervasive obsession with technique will triumph, even within the churches. Unchallenged, the spirit of this age seeks to turn all mystery — including the final mystery of death — into spectacle or solution.

The twentieth-century Russian religious philosopher Nicholas

---

12. Ramsey, "Death's Pedagogy," p. 343. The phrase "sturgeon for dinner" is taken from Leo Tolstoy's great tale *The Death of Ivan Ilych*, which I will discuss in the chapters that follow.

Berdyaev once stated that "a system of ethics which does not make death its central problem has no value and is lacking in depth and earnestness."[13] Unless it makes death its central problem, Christian ethics runs the risk of mimicking other systems of ethics by focusing solely on the here and now and holding out the prospect of attaining complete happiness in this life. And yet, by focusing on temporal and transitory goods and values, these ethical systems actually tend to make us forgetful of death. But Christian faith is nourished by the dogmas of the crucifixion, resurrection, last judgment, and eternal life, and so, Berdyaev insisted, all valuation and judgment in a Christian ethics must begin with the fact that death claims every human being and would nullify every human effort to achieve happiness and meaningful existence were it not for the fact that Jesus Christ triumphed over death for our sakes through his own freely offered death on the cross.

The rise of Dr. Kevorkian and the thanatos syndrome in our culture validates Berdyaev's concern and adds even greater urgency to his challenge to Christian theologians and ethicists. Christian ethics favors life over death always, even if that life is near its end. But Christian faith does not attribute ultimate value to human life. The Christian assessment of the value of human life issues from the conviction that God has revealed in Jesus Christ his intention to save us all from sin and death. This conviction is buttressed by two strong corollaries — (1) that the death of the human person is not merely a phenomenon of nature and its cycles and (2) that after the fall the "natural" end to our temporal lives has been replaced by "corruptible death," which, apart from divine intervention, leads to the extinction of the individual. This contradicts the immortality that God originally intended for human beings.

Despite their rich ethical heritage, Christians today are increasingly uncertain about why the church has prohibited euthanasia.

13. Berdyaev, *The Destiny of Man* (New York: Harper & Row, 1960), p. 263.

They are not aware that the church offers a compelling alternative to the two extreme viewpoints that contend in the public arena today — the view that calls for all possible medical treatment even in the case of terminally ill and dying patients and the view that active euthanasia and physician-assisted suicide are morally permissible and ought to be legalized. The Christian ethic I embrace allows for careful moral calibration of the viability of a human life made in light of the best judgment of the physician. This ethic makes an important distinction between a deliberate taking of life and allowing to die — a distinction that must be supported theologically and reformulated for modern people. Killing a patient is morally wrong in all cases, but allowing the life of a patient to ebb and death to come is sometimes permissible. Human beings are created in the image and likeness of God, but human life is still only creaturely life and hence is invested with great but not ultimate value.

In its most profound catholic expression, Christian faith has consistently sought to discern ways to align human will and behavior with the divine will — in medicine as in other spheres of life, such as the family, the economic order, and the political state. Perhaps, as Paul Ramsey once conjectured, only such a faith is capable of establishing and adhering to the "conscionable category of 'ceasing to oppose death'" while also setting absolute limits on taking the lives of severely afflicted or terminally ill persons.[14] It may be in some cases that the best possible care, the care that is most consistent with divine care, will involve helping the dying to die as well as possible. Dr. Kevorkian and his allies, however, would have us forget the important distinction between killing and letting die and take the fateful step of playing god rather than obeying God in our conduct toward those among us whose perishing is near rather than distant.

14. Ramsey, *The Patient as Person* (New Haven: Yale University Press, 1970), p. 156.

Although euthanasia is always near the surface of the discussion in this book, it is not my sole concern here. I wrote this book because I believe that in recent years Christians have not said enough in explicitly theological ways about death, and I want to offer a response informed by biblical faith to the thanatos syndrome that is spreading both outside and inside the church. In Chapter 1, I review and analyze cultural attitudes toward death and the movement endorsing physician-assisted suicide. In Chapters 2 and 3, I undertake a theological discussion of death. And in Chapters 4 and 5, I offer explicitly Christian ethical reflection on caring for the dying.

Whatever the merits of speculative theologies of death, practical guides to Christian care for the dying, and books on grieving, I have not sought to take this book wholly in any of these directions. In my reading on the subject, I have found too few books that seek to bring together the concerns of theology and medicine, of faith and medical ethics, and it is this omission that I have sought to address here, bringing to bear both general Christian theological views and some insights specifically associated with Orthodox beliefs and practices. I sincerely hope that my efforts here will encourage others to expand the discussion in fruitful ways by further exploring the contributions that theology can make to our perspective on the issues.

I

The Culture of Death

I

Aversion and Obsession:
Reading the Pulse of the Culture

MOST Americans are familiar with Walt Disney's animated feature *Bambi*. Far fewer are familiar with the classic children's book upon which it is based, Felix Salten's *Bambi: A Life in the Woods*. The Disney version of the story is an archetypal American tale of romantic love, oozing with sentimentality. Salten's original, on the other hand, is a profound fable about living in the face of death without allowing it to rob life of hope or meaning. It speaks to the ways in which we in this culture hide death from view and refuse to deal seriously with it as a moral or metaphysical problem.

Salten tells the story of a young buck named Bambi who comes under the tutelage of a mysterious, solitary old stag. The stag shows Bambi how to live independently and always be alert to the dangers of the forest. "We must learn to live and be cautious," says the stag.[1] Man, the hunter with his gun, is the greatest threat to the woodland animals. For all of the other creatures, including Bambi's mother, he symbolizes death and inspires awe and dread so deep that the animals rarely mention those who have perished by his hand.

The stag, however, is not crippled by this fear. He has taken

1. Salten, *Bambi: A Life in the Woods* (New York: Minstrel Books, 1988), p. 162.

3

careful measure of human beings, and while he is fully acquainted with their capacity to unleash lethal force, he knows that man is neither omnipotent nor immortal. As Bambi grows to become a buck, the stag instructs him and passes along his wisdom, including the sure knowledge that there is a transcendent and providential Being who is greater even than man. One day the old stag leads Bambi to the still and bloodied body of a dead poacher.

> "Do you see, Bambi," the stag went on, "Do you see how He's lying there dead, like one of us? Listen, Bambi. He isn't all-powerful as they say. Everything that lives and grows doesn't come from Him. . . . Do you understand me Bambi?" asked the old stag.
>
> "I think so," Bambi said in a whisper.
>
> "Then speak," the old stag commanded.
>
> Bambi was inspired, and said trembling, "There is Another who is over us all, over us and over Him."
>
> "Now I can go," said the old stag.[2]

Death and the Loss of the Transcendent

The woods in which we live are likewise filled with demons of violence and death that terrify and stultify the lives of many people. Twenty-five years ago, Arthur McGill judged that our society was moving rapidly toward a post-Christian era, that people were abandoning their belief in a creative, nurturing, and redemptive reality that overarches their lives and beginning to "see the world as filled with shapeless ferocities that come and go."[3] Indeed, death has

2. Salten, *Bambi,* pp. 187-88.
3. McGill, *Suffering: A Test of Theological Method* (Philadelphia: Westminster Press, 1982), p. 50.

increasingly come to overshadow all of life in our culture; we are gripped by anxiety in the face of the untreatable diseases and random violence that threaten to snatch away our health and our lives.

Many people in our society have cut their ties to the sort of larger sacral context that has traditionally assigned meaning to the experiences associated with illness and dying. Apart from these sacral structures, many have difficulty dealing with such painful experiences. Every day they are exposed to reports of divorce, spousal battery, and the physical and sexual abuse of children. Every day they encounter stories of the violence occurring all around them — burglaries, holdups, muggings, rapes, murders, riots, genocidal wars. They hear incessant warnings about the depletion of the ozone layer, pesticides in their food, radon in their basements, asbestos in their schools, secondhand cigarette smoke in their workplace, and countless other noxious and invisible threats surrounding them. And every week a new batch of experts crowds the talk-show circuit to describe the latest physical and psychological maladies. After long exposure to this barrage of bad news, many are gripped with a fear that they are poised precariously on the edge of an abyss, completely surrounded by destructive and lethal powers. They have become convinced that ultimately life itself is arbitrary and absurd. The best that many can hope for in the face of this constant threat of suffering and death is the protection offered by advanced medical technology — but that has turned out to be a mixed blessing. Increasingly people are as reluctant to surrender themselves entirely to the physicians and the dehumanizing machinery of medicine as they are to surrender themselves to disease. And even if medical treatment is effective in restoring them to health, many people come away from the treatment feeling defeated on some level, newly convinced that they remain at the mercy of both the microbes and the medical technicians.

In his novel *The Poorhouse Fair,* John Updike presents his readers with Connor, an administrator of a home for the elderly who believes that it is his special calling to protect people from the surrounding destructive powers. He ridicules traditional religious faith and its claim that suffering and death have meaning. Hook, one of the old people under his care, a Southerner and Christian believer, argues against Connor's atheistic humanitarianism. He defends biblical theism and the belief that creation issues from the hands of a benevolent God and that life is good. Connor is unswayed: "People speak of loving life. Life is a maniac in a closed room."[4] He is Updike's version of Dostoevsky's Grand Inquisitor. The setting, however, is not the church of a sacral age but a total health care institution in a secular society. Connor believes that "Pain is evil" and that the home he runs is the only "heavenly" reward its wards will ever receive. Hook disagrees. "It is an error to believe that the absence of evil will follow from the elimination of pain," he says.[5] "There is no goodness, without belief. Only busyness. And if you have not believed, at the end of your life you shall know you have buried your talent in the ground of this world and have nothing saved to take into the next."[6] But in this post-Christian, postbiblical culture, Hook's convictions seem as timeworn and anachronistic as the old Southerner himself.

Aversion and Obsession

William F. May argues that death is the last sacral power in a post-Christian culture. Modern people avoid death "because they recognize in the event an immensity that towers above their resources for handling it. In effect, death (or the reality that brings

4. Updike, *The Poorhouse Fair* (New York: Fawcett Crest Books, 1958), p. 121.
5. Updike, *The Poorhouse Fair*, p. 115.
6. Updike, *The Poorhouse Fair*, p. 123.

it) is recognized as some sort of sacred power that confounds the efforts of man to master it."[7] In the modern American funeral home, the parlor in which the body rests is furnished as if it were a living room in anyone's home. The dead body is beautified; the face is made hardly recognizable with cosmetics that cover up death's pallor in order to leave the impression of life.

The effects of this denial and expulsion of death on our perceptions and expectations are sometimes quite bizarre. During a trip I made to Russia in the fall of 1991, the group I was with visited the parish church of Fr. Alexander Men, a charismatic Orthodox priest who, only a year before, had been brutally axed to death — many believed by agents of the KGB. The small wooden church was crowded with Sunday worshipers and pilgrims who had come to pay homage at this holy site of a modern-day martyr. Like many Orthodox churches, this one had no pews. Everyone stood, and in the middle of this crush of people lay an open casket that displayed the body of an old babushka. People occasionally made their way up to the casket, touching and kissing the wrinkled and shrunken old woman. After a time, an Episcopal priest who was standing next to me whispered: "Is it a common practice to place such mannequins in Orthodox churches?" This clergyman in his sixties who had buried many people during his lifetime simply could not see death in front of him when it had not been disguised, sanitized, and set apart from real life.

We needn't look very far to observe sillier but no less telling examples of denial and aversion in the face of death. In the winter of 1994, the *Baltimore Sun* ran a wire story entitled "'Dead End' Dead in Sensitive Colorado City" that underscores our uneasiness with anything that even reminds us of death. "Signs warning of

---

7. May, "The Sacral Power of Death in Contemporary Experience," in *On Moral Medicine: Theological Perspectives in Medical Ethics,* ed. Stephen E. Lammers and Allen Verhey (Grand Rapids: William B. Eerdmans, 1987), p. 175.

dead-end streets apparently are too macabre for some people," the article explained, "so the City Council [of Longmont, Colorado] voted to replace them with less sensitive panels reading 'no outlet.'" One resident who favored the change was quoted as saying, "We just moved into a condo, right outside there's a dead-end sign. . . . Every time you come, you have to go by this sign, and it just isn't very pleasant."

When I read this story I couldn't help recalling John Cheever's hilarious and sardonic tale "The Death of Justina." The protagonist, who has the suspiciously symbolic name of Moses, discovers his wife's old cousin Justina "sitting on the living-room sofa [in his home] with a glass of good brandy, [having] breathed her last."[8] Moses meets one obstacle after another as he tries to arrange for the removal of Justina's body from the house for a proper burial. He learns that several years earlier, in order to stop a funeral home from being built in the neighborhood, the town passed a zoning regulation making it illegal either to die or to be buried in Proxmire Manor. Thus, Moses is unable to obtain the death certificate for Justina that the undertaker requires in order to transport the dead body. The mayor tells Moses that he cannot make an exception to the rule because that would set a bad precedent. "People don't like to live in a neighborhood where this sort of thing goes on all the time," he explains.[9] Moses does eventually manage to get Justina's body taken to a funeral home, however, and Cheever grants him the honor of having the last word:

> The dead are not, God knows, a minority, but in Proxmire Manor their unexalted kingdom is on the outskirts, rather like a dump, where they are transported furtively as knaves and scoundrels and

8. Cheever, "The Death of Justina," in *The Stories of John Cheever* (New York: Ballantine Books, 1980), p. 507.
9. Cheever, "The Death of Justina," p. 513.

where they lie in an atmosphere of perfect neglect. Justina's life had been exemplary, but by ending it she seemed to have disgraced us all. *How can people who do not understand death hope to understand love, and who will sound the alarm?*[10]

Pornography and the Obsession with Death

While people in our culture have demonstrated a clear aversion to thoughts of death, they have also demonstrated an almost compulsive fascination with it. Who that saw them can forget the pictures of Rock Hudson taken in 1985 as he was being transferred on a stretcher from a privately chartered Boeing 747 to an awaiting ambulance, his face, a once-vital icon of masculine good looks, reduced by AIDS to a cadaverous death mask. English sociologist Geoffrey Gorer has shown how both our aversion to and obsession with death are manifested in a new kind of pornography. Gorer contends that that pornography is a "concomitant of prudery. . . . In contrast to obscenity, which is chiefly defined by situation, prudery is defined by subject; some aspect of human experience is treated as inherently shameful or abhorrent."[11] The Victorians dealt with sex this way, and despite our culture's presumptions about sexual liberation, sex remains a potent taboo for us as well. But death has edged out sex to become our preeminent taboo, says Gorer. "The natural processes of corruption and decay have become disgusting, as disgusting as the natural processes of birth and copulation were a century ago."[12] In recent years, so-called sex thrillers like *Fatal Attraction* and *Basic Instinct* and erotic horror movies like

10. Cheever, "The Death of Justina," p. 515.
11. Gorer, *Death, Grief, and Mourning* (Garden City, N.Y.: Doubleday, 1965), p. 195.
12. Gorer, *Death, Grief, and Mourning,* p. 196.

Interview with the Vampire have exploited this phenomenon. These movies combine death with sex, pandering to the subterranean desire of audiences to flirt with these two great modern taboos without risking guilt, grief, or embarrassment. In *Basic Instinct* (the prototype of many such films), orgasm and murder occur in the same bed, as the woman, like the female praying mantis, kills and consumes the male lover.

The earmark of pornography, Gorer continues, is its hallucinatory and delusory character. Private fantasies extrude into public expression intended for popular consumption. The 1990s have reaped a harvest of art that fits this description. In reporting on a major European art exhibit held in 1993, Paul Griffiths, an art critic for the *New Yorker,* noted that "if there is a single stylistic tic that fills both the pavilions and the work of the younger artists . . . it is the display of death, decay, and violence." Griffiths describes the work of several artists, including Jean-Pierre Reynaud's floor tiles of "thousands of unvarying images of skulls" and American artist Andres Serrano's exhibit "The Morgue," which displays "huge photographs of corpses." "Other than death," writes Griffiths, "the set subject is sex . . . with lots of genital imagery."[13]

As Freud understood, death and sex are deeply intertwined in the human psyche, perhaps pathologically among modern people. Our fascination with sex is a form of our fascination with death. So we can explain in Freudian terms why modern moviemakers have turned to the sex thriller and contemporary artists choose sex and death for their subjects. Sex and erotic love point to a union and communion often frustrated by egoism, pride, lust, and a proclivity for violence. But sexual orgasm and its aftermath of exhaustion and impotence are also reminders of death. Ruth, the down-and-out prostitute with whom Harry Angstrom adulterously cohabits in

13. Griffiths, "Titian in Paris: The Venice Biennial," *The New Yorker,* 2 August 1993, p. 70.

John Updike's early novel *Rabbit, Run,* tells Harry after their love-making that orgasm "is like falling through." Harry asks Ruth, "Where do you fall to?" She answers, "Nowhere." Later in the novel Ruth says to Harry, "You're Mr. Death himself."[14]

Denial of Death, Denial of Life

Fear and anxiety about death should not be confused with aversion to death. In his seminal study *Western Attitudes toward Death,* Philippe Ariès explains the difference. In earlier Western societies where Christianity dominated, death was very much a part of life, Ariès observes. For a variety of reasons involving social organization and the primitive state of medicine, death was a near and familiar occurrence. People died at home in the company of family and friends. Then as now, death could be ugly, messy, and tragic, and it was certainly feared and respected, but on the whole people were neither as repulsed nor as terrified by death as are modern folk. In part, the frequency and immediacy of death rendered it less alien and hence less threatening, but it was also the case that religion and belief in an afterlife, supported by familiar rituals of dying and mourning, enabled people to cope with death better as a part of living. According to Ariès, earlier Western culture did not make as strong a distinction as contemporary culture does "between the time before and the time after, this life and the afterlife. . . . On both sides of death, one is still very near the deep wellspring of sentiment."[15]

At the close of the movie *Forrest Gump,* Forrest stands by the grave of his deceased wife and says, "Momma always said that dyin'

---

14. Updike, *Rabbit, Run* (New York: Ballantine Books, 1960), pp. 83, 279.

15. Ariès, *Western Attitudes toward Death: From the Middle Ages to the Present,* trans. Patricia M. Ranum (Baltimore: The Johns Hopkins University Press, 1974), p. 104.

was a part of life. I sure wish it wasn't." Throughout the film, Forrest demonstrates a fundamental wisdom in response to the events in his life despite his I.Q. of 75. He experiences truth deeply and suffers from it when it is hard. Perhaps it is because he's "not a smart man" that Forrest can't dodge the truth the way the rest of us can. He wishes it wasn't so that death is a part of life, but he knows his Momma is right — death and dying are in the very midst of life and living. Forrest's religious beliefs are never defined in the film, but he does seem to express an implicit belief in life after death when he talks to his wife at her grave and delivers a note from their son to her. There is no reason to think that Forrest doesn't believe that his Jenny can hear him when he talks to her, since he means pretty much everything else he says in the film literally. In talking about his grief to his wife, he uses the same tone as he did in conversations with her when she was alive. But this last communication amounts to a religious act in that it hints of a real communion that transcends death. Forrest clearly remains near the wellspring of sentiment on both sides of death. It is less clear whether he has received any of the comforts that traditional Christian belief offers in these circumstances. While it is inarguably the case that death is a part of life insofar as it takes place in the midst of the living, it is also the case that death has been transformed into a passage toward a transcendent destiny that replaces the sting of separation with the joy of presence.

I would not uncritically lament the loss of the religious manner in which our ancestors tamed or domesticated death. There are both good and bad things that might be said about that. Nonetheless, two points that Ariès makes about the history of death in Western culture are especially helpful in thinking about a contemporary theological ethic of death and dying. First, in the modern era, "despite the apparent continuity of themes and ritual," death is "furtively pushed out of the world of familiar things."[16] Even self-consciously religious

16. Ariès, *Western Attitudes toward Death*, p. 105.

people tend to respond to death with an other-worldliness that suggests a weakened belief in Providence and no real sense of grace. Second, vast numbers of contemporary people have difficulty making anything good out of the process of dying and death itself. And all that remains for many mourners today is a vague hope that they are sending the deceased to some "far off" better place. By the nineteenth century, argues Ariès, even within the family that "believed in the afterlife . . . death became the unaccepted separation, the death of the other, 'thy death,' the death of the loved one."[17]

Ariès argues that more and more modern people react against this sort of other-worldly piety by embracing a one-dimensional this-worldly secularism. In the end, however, this makes little difference: like its weak religious counterpart, the secular outlook is typically characterized by dread of death and propensity to expel it from the world of the living. "Thus death gradually assume[s] another form, both more distant and more dramatic, more full of tension."[18] Death becomes unnamable. "Everything henceforth goes on as if neither I nor those who are dear to me are any longer mortal," says Ariès. "Technically, we admit that we might die; we take out insurance . . . to protect our families from poverty. But really, at heart we feel we are non-mortals. And surprise! Our life is not as a result gladdened!"[19]

The Rise of the New Therapeutic Naturalism

Today new answers are being proposed for the old problem of death. The modern therapists of death and dying are trying hard

17. Ariès, *Western Attitudes toward Death*, p. 106.
18. Ariès, *Western Attitudes toward Death*, p. 106.
19. Ariès, *Western Attitudes toward Death*, p. 107.

to transmute the secular view of death left in the wake of the decline of traditional religion into an acceptance of death as something quite natural. Sherwin B. Nuland's recent best-seller *How We Die* is an exceptionally sensitive and compelling expression of this project. Nuland relates stories from his life as a physician to show the reader how the banishment of death — real death, not the Hollywood variety — demeans and devalues life, and he sharply criticizes the medical profession for having become an accomplice in this denial of death. In 1950, Nuland notes, 50 percent of American deaths happened in hospitals; today that figure has reached 80 percent. Death is thus moving out of the field of vision of most Americans, moving behind the curtains and the banks of medical equipment. "The cultural symbolism of sequestering the dying," says Nuland, "is here as meaningful as the strictly clinical perspective of improved access to specialized facilities, and for most patients even more so. The solitary death is now . . . well recognized."[20] Nuland contends that people who die in this way, isolated from most aspects of their life prior to illness and hospitalization and adrift in the unfamiliar environment of modern medical treatment, will have a more difficult time finding meaning in the experience of dying.

To his credit, Nuland recognizes that much of what goes on in medicine today demonstrates how much we have been stripped of traditional religious and moral resources for facing death without loss of hope or meaning. In many cases, the art of caring for the dying has given way to an art of saving life at all cost. He adds that this new science of saving life is mostly concerned with the physician's need to be in control and the patient's need to feel that someone is in control. For the doctor who internalizes or flaunts the image of the physician as shaman or soldier, "even a temporary

20. Nuland, *How We Die: Reflections on Life's Final Chapter* (New York: Alfred A. Knopf, 1993), p. 255.

victory justifies the laying waste of the fields in which a dying man has cultivated his life."[21]

This is good stuff. But in the end I disagree with Nuland's naturalism. He sums up his ethic near the end of *How We Die:*

> A realistic expectation also demands our acceptance that one's allotted time on earth must be limited to an allowance consistent with the continuity of the existence of our species. Mankind, for all its unique gifts, is just as much a part of the ecosystem as any other zoolic or botanical form, and nature does not distinguish. We die so that the world may continue. We have been given the miracle of life because trillions upon trillions of living things have prepared the way for us and then have died — in a sense, for us. We die, in turn, so that others may live. The tragedy of a single individual becomes, in the balance of natural things, the triumph of ongoing life.[22]

Nuland tries to give meaning back to death and dying with this naturalism, and I do not discount the possibility that some of his audience may be persuaded. Certainly it is to Nuland's credit that he makes a case for practicing medicine in a way that is calibrated to the personal needs of dying patients. But his naturalism is a two-edged sword. It may rightly criticize modern medicine's betrayal of the patient's need for meaning in the process of dying, but it can also undercut the value of personal life — and in doing so open the way for managed death and state-managed experimentation on the dying. In the passage just cited, we find Nuland shifting his concern away from the individual to the survival of the species and the ecosystem, reducing the human being to an epiphenomenon of the natural order and thus depersonalizing death.

21. Nuland, *How We Die*, p. 265.
22. Nuland, *How We Die*, p. 267.

What Nuland reveals about his personal history and sensibilities suggests that he would likely be opposed to Dr. Kevorkian's new science of obitiatry, but there is nothing in the sort of naturalism he propounds that is incompatible with such experimentation.

The Culture of Death

Our deep aversion to and obsession with death in contemporary Western culture attest to its power over us. Indeed, it has become our preeminent taboo, and many of us have come to view it as an ultimate power, a godlike thing. Yet, as with all things we fashion into gods, we have managed to overcome our fear of death enough to seek to manipulate it for our own purposes, to summon it to provide a solution for our personal and social problems. We have overcome our aversion to death enough to get comfortable with using it to get rid of criminals, to end unwanted pregnancies, and, increasingly, to relieve the misery of illness and injury. Through our own choices and predilections, we have fashioned a culture of death.[23]

Many secular moderns remain unaware of the fact that they are submerged in this culture of death. The contemporary secular imagination typically prides itself on its affirmation of life and is quick to dismiss the biblical imagination as morbid and other-worldly. But in fact, the secular imagination is formed by fictional and nonfictional stories that leave the impression — even the conviction — that death lurks everywhere and encompasses all of life, whereas the biblical imagination is formed by stories in which death

23. In the following discussion of the culture of death, I develop a number of important insights mined from Peter J. Rega, "The Culture of Death," *Baltimore Sun,* 13 December 1994, p. 19A.

is subject to a God who redeems his sin-damaged creation and renders death a contingent rather than an ultimate reality.

Secular moderns cling to the belief that they can celebrate life at the same time they embrace a culture of death. Some argue that they can best embrace life by putting an end to the lives they no longer value. But in making such a determination, they do not give enough consideration to the darkness that death casts over life whatever the use to which it is put. In *Rabbit, Run,* John Updike describes Harry Angstrom as someone "who has no taste for the dark, tangled, visceral aspect of Christianity, the *going through* quality of it, the passage *into* death and suffering that redeems and inverts these things, like an umbrella blowing inside out."[24] Moderns flirt with death as an answer to their problems, but, like Harry Angstrom, they refuse to look directly at death and see the darkness. They are unwilling to face the truth about sin and evil, unwilling to acknowledge that it is beyond the power of the physician, abortionist, euthanist, or executioner to provide the cure and the salvation they really seek.

Updike says that Harry Angstrom lacks "the mindful will to walk the straight line of paradox. His eyes turn toward the light however it glances into his retina."[25] The faith that Harry yearns for demands that he be honest about his mortal condition and willing to give himself up to God's care. Then he might begin to experience grace and have hope even when death intrudes. Living in the 1950s, Harry is not yet a child of the post-Christian era, and he still finds some traces of his Lutheran upbringing influencing his reaction when his wife accidentally drowns their baby daughter. It is darkly ironic that the child died in water, for "it occurs to him, what no one has mentioned, [that] the child was never baptized."[26] Harry fears that the death of his daughter holds no promise of salvation. I take this message from

24. Updike, *Rabbit, Run,* p. 218.
25. Updike, *Rabbit, Run,* p. 218.
26. Updike, *Rabbit, Run,* p. 269.

Updike's story: if more people faced death in the presence of God as Harry does at just this moment, they might begin to recover from the thanatos syndrome. At least there might be fewer abortions, fewer executions, fewer homicides, and a greater reluctance to turn to physician-assisted suicide and euthanasia as solutions to the problems of chronic pain and terminal illness. Sadly, Harry turns away from his tentative encounter with God and (as we find in *Rabbit Redux*) goes back to Ruth for sex and escape. Sadly, too, our society is likewise turning away from any sort of encounter with God at virtually every critical juncture and choosing instead the thanatos syndrome and the embrace of redemptionless death.

Conclusion

The attitudes toward death in contemporary Western society pose a serious challenge to traditional Christian teaching on the subject. To the extent that these attitudes have infiltrated the Christian community, they have provoked a crisis of faith for many. Even among those who profess to have a biblical faith there is confusion about the meaning of death. Death is becoming the ultimate concern of all those who lack the mediation of the sacred and transcendent in their lives, religious and nonreligious people alike. Such people tend to fall into slavery either to a stultifying and debilitating dread of death or to the comforting illusion that life is for the living and death is for the dying. They become victims of a great spiritual emptiness. I do not believe that humanistic naturalism of the sort proposed by Sherwin Nuland is capable of calming these deep fears, reversing the denial, or filling the emptiness. But I do believe that a Christian theological vision of death can offer the meaning for which we yearn as we face both life and death, and it is to this vision that we will turn in the next two chapters.

II

The Christian Vision
of Death

2

Love and Death

How can a people who do not mean to understand death hope to understand love, and who will sound the alarm?

John Cheever, "The Death of Justina"

The fathers assert that perfect love is sinless. And it seems to me that in the same way a perfect sense of death is free from fear.

St. John Climacus, *The Ladder of Divine Ascent*

IN THIS and the following chapter we will consider the Christian vision of death in preparation for a look at a practical ethic of caring for the dying. I want to start this consideration by exploring an aspect of death that is familiar to virtually all human beings — namely, death's parasitic relationship to love. Death would not be so bitter were it not that love makes life so sweet. Nor would death inspire such fear and dread were it not that it cuts us off from those whom we love and who love us. Love creates communion and produces joy, but death can throw us into desolation and despair.

Death and the Faith that Sustains Love

When death steals someone or something from us that we love, it tempts us to despair of life. But Christianity warns that despair over death and dying is a sign and source of sin, just as surely as sin and death are related. The weakness of the flesh is both a symptom and an outward sign of a failure to trust in the love of God and his lordship over life. Death's grip on life has deep roots and profound consequences involving much more than just the end of our physical existence. In the absence of faith, death gains strength and destructive power over life. It weighs us down with the suspicion that love and communion with others may not be real and that life might not be worth living. Death makes its home in the very midst of life like the rot that spoils fruit.

Our lives are filled with countless little intimations of death. When human feelings wane and disappear, "this is an experience of death," wrote Nicholas Berdyaev. "When . . . we part with a person, a house, a garden, an animal, and have the feeling that we may never see them again, this is an experience of death. The anguish of every parting, of every severance in time and space, is the very experience of death."[1] Berdyaev's observations help to explain why so few people are convinced or comforted by the assertion of legions of modern therapists and specialists that death is natural and ought to be graciously accepted as part of living. As the Lutheran theologian Helmut Thielicke has said, "Practically, death makes a mockery of any consolation from biological or idealistic" theories that insist that death is natural or that it does not threaten the meaning of living. "Practically, no one experiences the end of life the same way as life itself, as if they were seamlessly joined. . . . Thus we can maintain that as a practical matter anxiety about the end of life stands in real contradiction to any theoretical explanation of death

---

1. Berdyaev, *The Destiny of Man* (New York: Harper & Row, 1960), p. 251.

as natural. Here it must be said that anxiety is still anxiety, even when it is suppressed behind clenched teeth or when it takes refuge in an ideological scheme of immortality."[2]

Both Berdyaev and Thielicke believe that human nature is a unity of physical and spiritual existence. Human beings obviously have a biological nature like that of all other living things. Yet human beings are also persons created in the image and likeness of God, loved by God as such, and destined by God to immortality. We are conscious and self-conscious beings who reflect the triune identity of God and realize the fullness of our own identity only in loving relationships with others. When death destroys these relationships, we are diminished.

In *A Grief Observed,* upon which the recent and highly acclaimed movie *Shadowlands* was based, the great twentieth-century Christian apologist C. S. Lewis explores with ruthless self-honesty his personal struggle to hold on to his faith after the death of his wife, Joy. For most of his adult years, C. S. Lewis had written masterfully of the great doctrinal footholds of Christianity and made a case for these Christian tenets with reference to the ordinary lives of his lay readers. Death, however, caught up with Lewis in a way that none of his writing had quite prepared him for. Death took away from him the greatest love of his life and stung him with desolation and despair. "Thought after thought, feeling after feeling, action after action, had H. for their object," he wrote. "Now their target is gone. . . . So many roads lead thought to H. I set out on one of them. But now there's an impassable frontier-post across it. So many roads once; now so many *culs de sac*."[3]

2. Thielicke, *Death and Life,* trans. Edward H. Schroeder (Philadelphia: Fortress Press, 1970), p. 14.

3. C. S. Lewis, *A Grief Observed* (1961; reprint, New York: Bantam Books, 1976), p. 55. Subsequent references to this book will be made parenthetically in the text.

Some have argued that Lewis lost his faith during this time of grieving. I disagree. But there is no question that Lewis's faith was changed by the experience. I believe that it was transplanted into the soil of a Christian realism about death that was missing in his earlier apologetical writing. Now he reported the awful desolation and pain of separation by death in his own life.

> I have been thinking of H. and myself as peculiarly unfortunate in being torn apart. But presumably all lovers are. She once said to me, "Even if we both died at exactly the same moment, as we lie here side by side, it would be just as much a separation as the one you're so afraid of." (Pp. 14-15)

> I had my miseries, not hers; she had hers, not mine. The end of hers would be the coming-of-age of mine. We were setting out on different roads. This cold truth, this terrible traffic-regulation ("You, Madam, to the right — you, Sir, to the left") is just the beginning of the separation which is death itself. (P. 14)

Near to despair, Lewis seriously entertained the possibility that if there is a God he might be malevolent rather than benevolent. "Someone said, I believe, 'God always geometrizes.' Supposing the truth were 'God always vivisects?' " (p. 33). But whether or not God exists or is a malevolent rather than a benevolent being was not, in any case, the most immediate and gnawing question for Lewis. The real issue was death. For death certainly is real, as real as the devastating absence of a loved one. "It is hard to have patience with people who say, 'There is no death,' or 'Death doesn't matter,' " he wrote. "You might as well say that birth doesn't matter" (p. 16). And what does death do? It removes the presence of the beloved. Did this mean that his beloved Joy was no more and that the love they shared was only an illusion? Lewis would not tolerate that conclusion.

If H. "is not," then she never was. I mistook a cloud of atoms for a person. There aren't, and never were, any people. Death only reveals the vacuity that was always there. What we call the living are simply those who have not yet been unmasked. All equally bankrupt, but some not yet declared. But this must be nonsense; vacuity revealed to whom? bankruptcy declared to whom? (Pp. 32-33)

Earlier in his life, Lewis might have built a rational case for Christianity on this sort of deductive logic and simply passed over the existential problem. But the death of his wife made the existential problem paramount and redirected his attention to the great mystery of God's purposes in death.

The mystical union [of the dead in Christ] on the one hand. The resurrection of the body, on the other. I can't reach the ghost of an image, a formula, or even a feeling, that combines them. But the reality, we are given to understand, does. Reality the iconoclast once more. Heaven will solve our problems, but not, I think, by showing us subtle reconciliations between all our apparently contradictory notions. The notions will all be knocked from under our feet. We shall see that there never was any problem . . . that some shattering and disarming simplicity is the real answer. (Pp. 82-83)

But the real answer remains on the other side of death; the living are left to deal with the mystery and the pain of loss. Death either sends us back to the faith that reveals the true Source of life which overcomes death or it robs us of all hope and any reason to go on living.

Love and Death

A Grief Observed gives us some firsthand insights into the ways in which death is parasitic on love. Love naturally desires an everlasting relationship with the beloved and hence the immortality of the beloved. Death thwarts this desire. Moreover, the death of those we love foreshadows our own demise. Death stalks us and draws ever nearer through their deaths. Death weakens the superstructure of life by creating pockets of emptiness within it — pockets of emptiness that are quick to accommodate desolation and despair.

St. Augustine's lamentation in the *Confessions* over the death of his boyhood friend is perhaps the most famous literary expression of the hurt that death inflicts when it tears the people we love from our lives.

> My heart was black with grief. Whatever I looked upon had the air of death. . . . I was at once utterly weary of life and in great fear of death. It may be that the more I loved him the more I hated and feared, as the cruelest enemy, that death which had taken him from me; and I was filled with the thought it might snatch away any man as suddenly as it had snatched him.[4]

St. Augustine dug deeply into the mysterious existential relationship of love and death. Death is dreadful, he concluded, not only because it foreshadows our own personal extinction but because even before that it steals from us the sweet communion of friendship.

> I wondered that other mortals should live when he was dead whom I had loved as if he would never die; and I marveled still

4. Augustine, *The Confessions of St. Augustine*, trans. F. J. Sheed (New York: Sheed & Ward, 1943), pp. 66, 67-68 (4:4, 5-6).

the more that he should be dead and I his other self living still. Rightly has a friend been called "the half of my soul." For I thought of my soul and his soul as one soul in two bodies; and my life was a horror to me because I would not live halved. And it may be that I feared to die lest thereby he should die wholly whom I had loved so deeply.[5]

According to Augustine and all the great Christian writers, death not only threatens to destroy our very *humanitas,* to tear asunder the personal unity of body and soul, but also rips apart the social fabric of our lives. Death violates both the dead and the living. A being created for immortality stares into the abyss of nothingness and recoils because love will not abide desolation and nothingness. Much more than the prospect of my own personal extinction is at stake, finally. The Christian belief in the resurrection is not merely a selfish assurance that the "I" will not perish. Jesus says that in his Father's house are many rooms (John 14:2). Love is the foundation and mortar of that many-roomed house. "Those who love me will keep my word, and my Father will love them, and we will come to them and make our home with them" (John 14:23).

On my first visit to Armenia in 1990, I visited the home of Anahid and Kevork Oynoyan. They had lost their twelve-year-old son, Armen, in the catastrophic earthquake of December 1988, and Kevork was profoundly depressed as a result. Late one evening, after the electricity had been cut off, Kevork and I sat at their small kitchen table lit by a solitary candle. He got up and brought back a copy of the New Testament and a book that had been distributed by the Hare Krishna sect describing the transmigration and reincarnation of the soul. He asked if I would explain the difference between reincarnation and the Christian belief in resurrection. He

5. Augustine, *The Confessions of St. Augustine,* p. 68 (4:6).

said that in his atheism classes years before he had been taught that Christianity is spiritualist. If that was so, weren't reincarnation and resurrection essentially the same?

I suggested that we read 1 Corinthians 15, where St. Paul defends the belief in the resurrection of the body and the soul. In silence, visibly and deeply absorbed, Kevork read that chapter not once but several times. Then joyfully he shouted, "So Christianity is materialist!" The darkness had lifted, because in St. Paul's teaching Kevork had discovered what he had hoped would be there but had not found in the book on reincarnation: the assurance that he would see his son again, recognize him, and be able to love him in an embrace of resurrected flesh. In the person of Jesus Christ, God's love is manifested as life. Jesus' resurrection proclaims the triumphant power of love and life over death.

The late Protestant theologian Joseph Haroutunian observed that more significant even than the anxiety induced by our consciousness "of the prospect of [our] physical dissolution" is the anxiety that "arises out of a love of life which is essentially a love of our fellowman and a love of ourselves as fellowmen."[6] Haroutunian maintained that this anxiety over the loss of fellow human beings is appropriate because it is a function not of egoism or of selfishness but of love: "A man dies as a fellowman, and the sting of death is his separation from his fellowmen, or the end of life which is the loss of fellowmen. It is love that provides the peculiar shock of human death, and the only way not to feel the sting of death is to deny the love which is our life."[7]

6. Haroutunian, "Life and Death among Fellowmen," in *The Modern Vision of Death,* ed. Nathan A. Scott Jr. (Richmond: John Knox Press, 1963), pp. 86, 88.
7. Haroutunian, "Life and Death among Fellowmen," p. 88.

The Loss of Love and the Denial of Death

In a culture where strong faith in the God of resurrection and life is no longer a source of hope and inspiration for many people, love seems also to fail. Anxiety about sickness and death is prefaced by the perception that love doesn't work anymore. Haroutunian points out this paradox: "We are concerned, almost neurotically concerned, about physical death because we are concerned about the failure of love. It is despair about love in our culture which generates despair about life."[8]

This despair is intimately bound up with how we view death. The ways in which we wage war against death in our society ironically make us accomplices in our own spiritual suicide. Consider our efforts to remove death from the moral sphere of the home and transfer it to the technological environment of the modern hospital, for example. To some extent, this development is a natural result of various social changes and advances in medical technology. But whatever the motives and inducements involved, it remains the case that our elaborate technologies often separate people from those whose love they need most of all when they are dying. And it is not only the dying who are deprived by this mechanization of medicine and institutionalization of death. Consciously or subconsciously, we all begin to anticipate in fear the same isolation and abandonment when our turn comes. We lose faith in love.

There is something utterly perverse at work in all of this. A trap has been laid. The more love we lose to death and separation, the more we fear our own mortality, and the more we fear our mortality, the more desperately we search for increasingly sophisticated technologies to combat or postpone death — and, of course, the increasingly sophisticated technologies only serve to isolate us yet more effectively from those we love when we most need their

8. Haroutunian, "Life and Death among Fellowmen," p. 92.

love. And yet we resist acknowledging the fact that no technology or therapy is capable of removing the sting of death from our lives. Only the love we are relinquishing to the false promises of technology and the new medicine is able to do this.

One last troubling aspect of this vicious circle of medicine and mortality is the extent to which we as a society are becoming increasingly insensitive to the terminally ill. Although we often deny it with clever rationalization, we are drawn to a reliance on medical technology at least in part because of our aversion to having to deal directly with death ourselves. When we commit our loved ones to modern medical treatment in the face of imminent death, we assure ourselves that we are doing so in order to secure the best available attention for them. But in doing so we are also ceding a burden of responsibility to the medical caregivers and distancing ourselves in other significant ways as well both from those we love and from the immediacy of death. In some proportion, we are exchanging love for separation, and this is a grave step to take. "A man who does not dread separation from his fellowman is not a wise man but a monster," notes Haroutunian. "The savor of death already makes him stink."[9] Any society that systematically ships the dying to hospitals and nursing homes is not so humane as it tries to believe.

In his great novels, Dostoevsky created many characters who are on the path to becoming monsters. They are usually homicidal or suicidal persons through whom Dostoevsky diagnosed the sickness of the modern soul. In *Crime and Punishment*, Svidrigaylov is a character who can certainly be said to stink of death. Many critics have argued that Svidrigaylov is the "Napoleanic personality" or Nietzschean superman who lives beyond good and evil that Raskolnikov, the protagonist of the novel, tries and fails to be. These critics describe Svidrigaylov as the nearly perfect incarnation of the demonic, a man who neither needs love nor has the capacity to love.

9. Haroutunian, "Life and Death among Fellowmen," pp. 88-89.

But I do not think Dostoevsky wanted to mark Svidrigaylov off so sharply from the rest of us.

Outwardly Svidrigaylov appears to be a respectable bourgeois gentleman; yet he rapes, drives those who work for him to kill themselves, and is responsible for the death of his wife. His desire to win the love and devotion of Rodin Raskolnikov's sister, Dunya, is colored by this perversity. Yet Svidrigaylov truly desires the love of Dunya: when she rejects his proposal of marriage, he commits suicide, blowing his brains out with a single shot from a revolver. What is the meaning of Svidrigaylov's suicide, and how would Dostoevsky have us judge it? First, Svidrigaylov is not unafraid of death. In this important respect, he proves not to be the Nietzschean superman. Second, Svidrigaylov's indifference about his cruelty toward others and his scant regard for the value of even his own life are marks of a monster. But why does he finally take his own life? Haroutunian's thesis about love and death offers an answer. Svidrigaylov commits suicide not in order to prove his superiority to the common lot of humanity but rather out of boredom with a life that seems to have no purpose other than indulgence in banal pleasures and entertainments of the flesh. He ends his life in despair that he has not managed to win the love that might have supplied his life with meaning. In this respect, he is in the vanguard of modern people living at the end of the age of faith. Svidrigaylov determines that it is his lot in life to be separated from his fellows, and, that being the case, he concludes that it makes no difference whether he is physically alive or dead.

Svidrigaylov himself poses to Raskolnikov the issue of whether he is a monster or merely one more casualty of a culture of disbelief:

That I had been pursuing a defenseless girl [Dunya] in my own house and humiliated her by my proposals — is that it? (You see, I'm taking the words out of your mouth!) But you have only to assume that I'm human, *et nihil humanum* — in a word, that I'm capable of being attracted and falling in love (which, of course, is something we can't help), and everything is explained in the most natural way. You see, the whole question is — am I a monster or am I myself the victim? What if I am a victim?[10]

One interpreter of this passage has commented that for Dostoevsky the "concept *homo sum, et nihil humanum a me alienum putu* ('I am a man and nothing human is alien to me') was for Dostoevsky a profoundly moral concept, implying the obligation squarely to confront human reality" and be responsible for one's fellow human being.[11] But Svidrigaylov twists the meaning of the phrase and uses it to excuse his own indifference to the suffering of self and others.

Svidrigaylov is a study in the banality of evil that excuses itself with a shrug and the assertion that that's just the way things are. The sentiment is echoed in a phrase all too common in our culture: "I'm only human!" The assumption is that to be human is to be a victim, a casualty of blind and essentially malevolent forces. Svidrigaylov would have us believe that both love and death are arbitrary. This is what I would call his "practical atheism." It is not so different from the attitude of people who excuse their indifference or avoidance of the suffering of others: "I can't help it that I have loved. Nor can I help it when I abandon even those whom I have loved because it hurts too much. People can't help it that they die. Nor can I help it that their dying is too much for me to bear. So it is better that I leave them in the care of others." Avoidance of judgment and responsibility is the hallmark of narcissism and an incipient nihilism. "Since love has failed me, I, in turn, abandon those whom I have loved when they require more from me than I can

10. Dostoevsky, *Crime and Punishment,* trans. David Magarshack (Harmondsworth: Penguin Books, 1951), pp. 296-97.
11. Robert Louis Jackson, "Philosophical Pro and Contra in Part I of *Crime and Punishment*," in *Fyodor Dostoevsky's "Crime and Punishment,"* ed. Harold Bloom, Modern Critical Interpretations Series (New York: Chelsea House, 1987), p. 69.

give. I feel empty and alone. I am myself a victim of indifference and the relentless pressures of daily living. How can I possibly help someone else when my own needs are not being met?" As increasing numbers of people relate to the world and others in this way, is it any surprise that more and more people take advantage of every opportunity to transfer responsibilities for the care of dying persons from themselves to accommodating doctors and nurses? William F. May notes that

> in the medieval church, as a priest and his assistants dragged a leper out of the church . . . and committed him to the lazar house, they would say to him: "And howsoever thou mayest be apart from the church and the company of the Sound, yet art thou not apart from the grace of God." [Now] . . . our implied address to the mad, the aged, and the criminal . . . [is]: "And howsoever thou mayest be apart from the community and the company of the Sound, yet art thou not apart from the ministrations of the Professional."[12]

A society that routinely commits its elderly and chronically and terminally ill members to institutional care away from loved ones is a society in jeopardy of losing its soul and becoming truly monstrous. There is, in fact, nothing more monstrous or deadly than shutting our fellow human beings off from love.

This brings us back to the question posed by John Cheever in "The Death of Justina": "How can people who do not mean to understand death hope to understand love, and who will sound the alarm?"[13] Contrary to what so many of the so-called experts on death tell us, death is not natural for human beings in the same way

12. May, *The Patient's Ordeal,* Medical Ethics Series (Bloomington, Ind.: Indiana University Press, 1991), p. 149.

13. Cheever, "The Death of Justina," in *The Stories of John Cheever* (New York: Ballantine Books, 1980), p. 515.

it is for God's other terrestrial creatures, and it is pointedly incompatible with love. Yet, in our fallen and sinful condition, we perceive the true meaning of love only when we understand the evil of death and vice versa. Death strikes a blow at the image of the triune God within us when it takes from us those whom we love and with whom we have shared our lives. Death even struck at the person of Jesus Christ, the Life of this world.

In his funeral oration on the death of his father, the great fourth-century theologian St. Gregory of Nazianzus observed that because of the Son of God's loving sacrifice on the cross, "Life and death, as they are called, apparently so different, are in a sense resolved into, and successive to, each other."[14] The Son's sacrifice and death on the cross was God's deepest and most profound act of love for humankind. The Father left his Son vulnerable to death for our sakes. The Son, whose love for his fellow human beings knows no limit, voluntarily gave himself up to death to accomplish salvation for all. The existential and personal surety of this saving act of God is contingent, however, on our serious and faithful meditation upon the cross.

But death is trivialized in the contemporary world, and the cross of Christ is being forgotten. Television and the movies bombard us with false images of death, while those among us who are truly dying are placed out of sight in hospitals and nursing homes. In "The Death of Justina" Cheever sends up this vast denial of death in our culture and shows how that denial reflects and contributes to our diminished capacity to love others steadfastly and lastingly.

---

14. Gregory of Nazianzus, Oration 18: "On the Death of His Father," in *A Select Library of Nicene and Post-Nicene Fathers of the Christian Church*, 2d ser., vol. 7 (New York: Christian Literature, 1894), p. 268.

The Remembrance and Pedagogy of Death

The great Christian writers and saints have spoken of how a deliberate and conscientious remembrance of death enables us to learn to live life in faith and faithfulness — a benefit that we obviously lose when we deny death and expel the dying from our sight. We would do well to ask ourselves how we might best remember our deaths so as to live our lives with faith in God and enduring love for our fellow humanity.

The Gospels provide an answer to this question. They teach us that Christ made death the goal of his life. Christ repeatedly reminded his disciples that his life was a living toward dying. "He took the twelve aside again and began to tell them what was to happen to him, saying, 'See, we are going up to Jerusalem, and the Son of Man will be handed over to the chief priests and the scribes, and they will condemn him to death'" (Mark 10:32-33). Christ's discipline of remembering his death clarified the purpose of his life and ensured that his death would be redemptive for others. And while the great ascetical fathers and spiritual writers of Christianity remind us that Christ's sacrifice is once and for all and need not be repeated by us — indeed cannot be repeated by us, since he was the only sinless human being — they do insist that we pay careful attention, nonetheless, to the lessons that Christ teaches about the remembrance of death.

"The unremitting remembrance of death is a powerful trainer of body and soul," noted St. Hesychios of Sinai. "Vaulting over all that lies between ourselves and death, we should always visualize it, and even the very bed on which we shall breathe our last, and everything connected with it."[15] The exercise of remembrance is

---

15. St. Hesychios, "On Watchfulness and Holiness," in *The Philokalia*, vol. 1, trans. and ed. G. E. Palmer, Philip Sherrard, and Kallistos Ware (London: Faber & Faber, 1970), p. 178.

held up as one of the cardinal Christian virtues. Yet the remembrance of death is almost wholly ignored by contemporary theologians and ethicists when they canvas the Christian virtues and even when they specifically discuss death. I submit that we need to recover this virtue because, as St. John Climacus says in a passage that he attributes to the anchorite Hesychios the Horebite, "No one who has acquired the remembrance of death will ever be able to sin." St. John Climacus also advises in *The Ladder of Divine Ascent* that,

> just as bread is the most necessary of all foods, so the thought of death is the most essential of all works. The remembrance of death brings labors and meditations, or rather, the sweetness of dishonor to those living in community, whereas for those living away from turbulence it produces freedom from daily worries and breeds constant prayer and guarding of the mind, virtues that are the cause and the effect of the thought of death.[16]

In his *Four Quartets,* T. S. Eliot turns to this theme of the remembrance of death in "East Coker," as he attempts to exorcise the demons of the wasteland and reorient the modern egocentric and narcissistic self toward God and an active love for others. He reminds us that "our only health is the disease" of sin and mortality,

> And that, to be restored, our sickness must grow worse.
>   The whole earth is our hospital . . .
> Wherein, if we do well, we shall
> Die of the absolute paternal care
> That will not leave us, but prevents us everywhere.[17]

---

16. St. John Climacus, *The Ladder of Divine Ascent,* trans. Colm Luibheid and Norman Russell (New York: Paulist Press, 1983), pp. 134, 132.

17. Eliot, *Collected Poems, 1909-1962* (New York: Harcourt, Brace, Jovanovich, 1963), pp. 187-88.

Baptism and the Remembrance of Death

Baptism is the symbolic beginning of the Christian's remembrance of death and a point of reference for it through the rest of life. The great twentieth-century Protestant theologian Karl Barth once stated, "To those who are not ignorant the sign of baptism speaks of death." He goes on to explain that "baptism bears witness to us of the death of Christ, where the radical and inexorable claim of God upon men triumphed. . . . The void brought into being by the death of Christ is filled with the new life which is the power of the Resurrection."[18]

St. Paul's instructions and admonitions about baptism and death in his Epistle to the Romans form the centerpiece of the church's theology of baptism. "Do you not know that all of us who have been baptized into Christ Jesus were baptized into his death? Therefore we have been buried with him by baptism into death, so that, just as Christ was raised from the dead by the glory of the Father, so we too might walk in the newness of life" (Rom. 6:3-4). Death settled in as a parasite of love in the "old man," but love triumphed over death in Christ, the "new man." That new man is born out of death in baptism. Thus, according to St. Paul, baptism is a remembrance of death forward from our new spiritual birth in the font and back from the future of resurrected life. This Christian "fact" of baptism transforms death and the "memory" of death. Through baptism we are embraced by God in love as his very sons and daughters.

The death that we die in baptism nullifies the spiritual power of corruptible death that issued from Adam's first sin. Baptism binds together Christians by their common participation in the death and resurrection of Christ. Nevertheless, in a fallen and faithless world,

---

18. Barth, *The Epistle to the Romans,* trans. Edward C. Hoskyns (Oxford: Oxford University Press, 1968), pp. 193, 195.

the twin scourges of the fear of death and the forgetfulness of death persist in profaning life and emptying it of hope and meaning. Christians dare not fail to practice the pedagogy of death. Forgetfulness of the dying and crucified Son of God leads to forgetfulness of the Father's infinite and all-forgiving love for his creatures. Forgetfulness of the dead whom we have loved is bound to grow into forgetfulness of the dying among us. And forgetfulness of the dead and the dying is a sure step toward forgetfulness of Christ and eternal life.

In Cheever's story, Moses remembers his dead brothers whose graves he has neglected: "I thought suddenly of the neglected graves of my three brothers on the mountainside and that death is a loneliness much crueler than any hinted at in life. The soul (I thought) does not leave the body but lingers with it through every degrading stage of decomposition and neglect, through heat, through cold, through the long winter nights when no one comes with a wreath or a plant and no one says a prayer."[19] Thus we see that Moses' struggle against the denial and forgetfulness of death marks the start of his spiritual reawakening.

Remembrance and Apatheia

In *A Grief Observed*, C. S. Lewis consciously struggles not to forget his deceased wife. In the midst of this struggle, he realizes that not just any form of remembering will do. For there are, in fact, forms of remembering that draw us even deeper into grief and despair. Lewis resolves that he must not cling morbidly to leftover images of his wife nor become distracted by new fantasies of what she was like or what he might have been for her. "The earthly beloved, even

19. Cheever, "The Death of Justina," p. 506.

in this life, incessantly triumphs over your mere idea of her," he writes. "In that respect H. and all the dead are like God. In that respect loving her has become, in its measure, like loving Him. In both cases I must stretch out the arms and hands of love — its eyes cannot here be used — to the reality, through — across — all the changeful phantasmagoria of my thoughts, passions, and imaginings" (p. 77).

Lewis teaches an ancient lesson of Christian ascetical theology. If we are to remember the dead and dying in a way that is redemptive, our love for them needs to be fortified by the purest form of *agape*. Like the impassible love of God, our human love must be tempered with *apatheia*. This Christian *apatheia* is not the same as the negative Stoic ideals of passivity, detachment, and self-containment. Christian *apatheia,* rather, is the discipline of setting aside the passions and the distractions of the mind toward the goal of perfect communion in love. As Lewis says, this form of remembrance excludes "all the changeful phantasmagoria of my thoughts, passions, and imaginings." Freed of distraction, love can burn pure, the flame leaping out to the beloved "other." Christian *apatheia* is the self's movement out of itself toward ecstatic union with the other. Lewis describes this movement in reference to his wife's death: "We are 'taken out of ourselves' by the loved one while she is here. Then comes the tragic figure of the dance in which we must learn to be still taken out of ourselves though the bodily presence is withdrawn, to love the very Her, and not fall back to loving our past, or our memory, or our sorrow, or our relief from sorrow, or our own love" (p. 59). When we love and remember the dead this way, we also learn to love God; we prepare ourselves for the mystery of death and eternal life. And last but not least, this remembrance of death is an important exercise in helping us to love the dying in our midst even when they can no longer disclose their love for us.

Lewis shows us how we need the virtues of both *agape* and *apatheia* to cope with the death of loved ones. But the person who is dying and facing the prospect of separation from the ones she has loved through life has similar needs: she needs to learn not to cling to even the greatest of her earthly loves. She needs to practice *apatheia*. Then God will draw her up out of death into eternal life. In our act of dying, God beckons us one last time to relinquish all of our earthly loves and place them on the heavenly altar of his enduring love. If we redirect these loves toward God, as Christ did, then these loves needn't end in death, for God will raise them with us into eternal life. This is the meaning I glean from Lewis's startling remark at the end of *A Grief Observed*:

> How wicked it would be, if we could, to call the dead back! She said not to me but to the chaplain, "I am at peace with God." She smiled, but not at me. *Poi si tornò all' eterna fontana.* (P. 89)

3

The Vision of Death

DEATH IS as much of a mystery as life itself — a mystery that neither natural nor divine science is able to explain. As the Anglican theologian Austin Farrer so rightly said, "God does not give us explanations; he gives up a Son."[1] The Christian faith is not a theodicy; it provides no final rationale or explanation for death. At the core of the Christian vision of death lies Scripture's proclamation of salvation in Jesus Christ. Death is an evil that is defeated once and for all by the willing sacrifice of the Son of God on the cross and by his glorious resurrection and ascension to the right hand of the Father.

The twentieth-century Russian Orthodox theologian Georges Florovsky summed up the Christian realism about death when he wrote that "death is a catastrophe for man" and asserted that this is the foundational principle of Christian anthropology.[2] He held fast to the belief that death signifies the need for salvation — this in contrast to both the standard demythologized secular view of death

1. Farrer, "The Country Doctor," in *Austin Farrer: The Essential Sermons,* ed. Leslie Houlden (Cambridge, Mass.: Cowley Publications, 1991), p. 204.
2. Florovsky, *Creation and Redemption,* vol. 3 of *The Collected Works of Georges Florovsky* (Belmont, Mass.: Nordland Publishing, 1976), p. 111.

as the inevitable and ordinary end of personal existence and the reigning therapeutic view that we should accept death as perfectly natural and reconcile ourselves to our place in nature's cycle of birth, death, and new birth.

Alexander Schmemann, another contemporary Orthodox theologian, has pointed out the incompatibility of these secular views of death with the Christian faith. "It falsifies the Christian message to present and to preach Christianity as essentially life-affirming without referring this affirmation to the death of Christ and therefore to the very fact of death," Schmemann explained; it will not do "to pass over in silence the fact that for Christianity death is not only the end, but indeed the very reality of *this world*."[3]

The Christian vision of death affirmed and defended by Schmemann and Florovsky is rooted in Jesus' life and ministry, death and resurrection. Throughout his earthly ministry, wherever Jesus confronted sickness, he cured it, even to the point of bringing his friend Lazarus back from death. Through his crucifixion and resurrection, Jesus overcame death and made our lives immortal. These are the basic facts supporting the Christian vision of death.

Sin and Death

The classical Christian teaching is that death originated in the sin of Adam and Eve and spread to all of humankind, since all sinned (Rom. 5:12). St. Paul said that "the wages of sin is death" (Rom. 6:23) and "the sting of death is sin" (1 Cor. 15:56). This mystery is deeply and profoundly embedded in human personal and social reality and is not subject to scientific or empirical verification. Yet both common expe-

3. Schmemann, *For the Life of the World* (Crestwood, N.Y.: St. Vladimir's Seminary Press, 1973), p. 96.

rience and modern medical science tell us something about it. We have established statistical correlations between overeating (gluttony) and heart disease, sexual promiscuity and dangerous sexually transmitted diseases, and excessive drinking and liver disease, to name just a few. We are only beginning to realize how the stresses generated by various kinds of deception, vengefulness, and manipulation in the workplace and in the home can lead to a whole range of life-threatening illnesses. Where the vices rule, death draws near.

All of the great Christian writers since St. Paul have made essentially the same argument: sin and death are profoundly and mysteriously mixed together. The Orthodox Christian tradition grounds its theology of death in two core beliefs that expand on this Pauline teaching: (1) that the first couple was created with the potentiality for immortality and (2) that death as we know it in a fallen world is not the same thing as the natural cessation of life that Adam and Eve might have experienced had they not sinned.

The fifth-century Armenian catechismal text *The Teaching of Saint Gregory* comments on the creation story in Genesis 2 as follows: "Only the will of man . . . [is] independent to do whatever he wills. And he has been constrained in nothing more than what was warned: not to eat of the tree [Gen. 2:17], that thereby He [God] might make him worthy to receive greater things in return for lesser, and that by virtue of his having grace for his task, he might receive from the Creator, as recompense for lesser deeds, greater grace."[4] This early Christian catechism clearly identifies this "greater grace" with immortality. Had the first couple respected "the enviable God-given wisdom, through the observance of the command," they would have gone on

---

4. *The Teaching of Saint Gregory: An Early Armenian Catechism,* trans. Robert W. Thomson (Cambridge: Harvard University Press, 1970), pp. 45-46; italics mine. The catechism is included in *The History of the Armenians,* purported to be written by Agathangelos. The text of the catechism is attributed to Agathangelos by St. Gregory the Illuminator, who converted Tiridates, king of the Armenians, to Christianity in the early fourth century.

to enjoy "the inalienable glory of the existent one [God]."[5] The catechism distinguishes between creaturely temporality and the eternity of God: even before the fall, personal human life was destined to have a beginning and an end. But, had Adam and Eve not sinned, the "natural" cessation of their earthly lives would have been different from the death that results from sin, which is the only form of death that we are acquainted with. Had the first couple not succumbed to the temptation of the serpent in the garden, the cessation of their earthly existence would have marked a satisfactory completion and fulfillment of life and seen them through an uninterrupted passage into immortality with God.

The fall rendered the dying and death of human beings emblematic of failed and doomed existence. Contrary to God's desire, the first couple chose to live *out from themselves* and *back to themselves* rather than toward God, and human beings have behaved the same ever since. This is how humanity became subject to the natural law of death that, apart from divine intervention, permanently dissolves the individual organism into its elemental constituent parts. The Greek church fathers used the term "corruptible death" to describe the evil and abnormality of such a death for creatures whom God created in his own image and likeness. The early patristic writers generally agreed that death according to the natural law of the cessation and dissolution of an organism is a profoundly "unnatural" thing for human beings. Georges Florovsky summarized the patristic consensus about corruptible death as follows: "Strictly speaking, it is only man that dies. Death indeed is a law of nature, a law of organic life. But man's death means just this fall or entanglement into this cyclical motion of nature, just what ought not to have happened. . . . Only for man is death contrary to [human] nature and mortality is evil."[6] The anthem of St. John of Damascus in the

---

5. *The Teaching of Saint Gregory,* p. 48.
6. Florovsky, *Creation and Redemption,* p. 106.

Byzantine rite of burial describes vividly the ugly and humanly unnatural visage of corruptible death: "I weep and wail when I think upon death and behold our beauty, fashioned after the image of God, lying in the tomb disfigured, dishonored, bereft of form."[7]

Precisely because the human person is created in the image and likeness of divine personhood, human death amounts to more than mere animal death, even if it has a similar appearance. Human life — even sinful human life — amounts to more than the mere unfolding of a determinate nature. It is the enactment of a history marked by freedom of will. As we make the choices to determine our history, sin misdirects our will in ways that steer both our personal biography and our collective history toward dissolution and nothingness rather than into fullness of being in communion with God. That is the sense in which Florovsky speaks of human death becoming entangled in the entropy of natural existence. "In the generic life of dumb animals, death is . . . a natural movement in the development of the species; it is the expression rather of the generating power of life than infirmity. However, with the fall of man, mortality, even in nature, assumes an evil and tragic significance. . . . Death strikes at personality."[8]

Several patristic writers found support for this view of death in passages from the Wisdom of Solomon such as the following:

> God created us for incorruption,
> and made us in the image of his own eternity,
> but through the devil's envy death entered the world.
>
> (2:23-24)

St. Athanasius tendered perhaps the single most influential statement in the patristic tradition on the origin and nature of corruptible death in his small Christian classic *On the Incarnation*:

7. Cited by Florovsky in *Creation and Redemption*, p. 386.
8. Florovsky, *Creation and Redemption*, p. 106.

[God] brought them [Adam and Eve] into His own garden, and gave them a law: so that, if they kept the grace and remained good, they might still keep the life in paradise without sorrow or pain or care, *besides having the promise of incorruption in heaven;* but that if they transgressed . . . , they might know that *they were incurring that corruption in death which was theirs by nature.*"9

Thus, in Athanasius's view, dying into corruption involves more than "mere dying," because it presupposes sin and issues from it. Corruptible death is a sign of sin and judgment.

Now this is that of which Holy Writ also gives warning, saying in the Person of God: "Of every tree that is in the garden, eating thou shalt eat: but of the tree of the knowledge of good and evil, ye shall not eat of it, but on the day that ye eat, dying ye shall die." But by "dying ye shall die" what else could be meant than not dying merely, but also abiding ever in the corruption of death.10

Thus we can see that St. Athanasius and the Armenian *Teaching of St. Gregory* both maintain that the disobedience of Adam and Eve brought into existence a kind of death that would lead to extinction were it not for God's overriding intent for human beings to be immortal. The disobedience of the first human couple not only put

9. Athanasius, *On the Incarnation of the Word,* 3:4, in *A Select Library of the Nicene and Post-Nicene Fathers of the Christian Church,* 2d ser., vol. 4 (New York: Christian Publishing, 1892), p. 38; italics mine.

10. St. Athanasius, *On the Incarnation of the Word,* 3:5, p. 38. I have used this translation of *De Incarnatione Verbi Dei* because it is a more literal translation of Athanasius's own rather wooden translation of the Septuagint Greek text of Genesis 2:16. I don't want to get into a discussion here of whether Athanasius correctly understood the meaning of the phrase as it came to him through the Greek from the Hebrew. Suffice it to say that the interpretation of this text as he renders it has a long theological history that would make for an interesting study in and of itself.

immortality into jeopardy — one might say suspended it — but introduced what St. Paul called "the sting of death" (1 Cor. 15:56). Human experience is now suffused with the typically vague but sometimes acute sense that everything of value and joy in life is disintegrating and being despoiled. We all experience moments when the harmony of the body-and-soul union is assaulted or severely weakened, moments when our body or mind seems out of control and our identity and relationship with the world seem to be at risk. These descents into sickness are what dying in sin is ultimately about.[11]

As in the prayer of St. John of Damascus, death, as the dissolution of the union of body and soul, is described and lamented in the liturgies of the Orthodox churches. The Armenian burial service describes this corruptible death as having been summoned by God and "poured . . . out upon creatures, in order that the wickedness that had befallen might not remain immortal."[12] Note that the prayer does not say that God created death but rather that God allowed the sinful creature to lapse back into the elements out of which it was made. The Byzantine Orthodox tradition even includes a prayer that beseeches God to mercifully hasten this process of dissolution so that "the destructible bond" of body and soul might be dissolved — the body to "be dissolved from the elements of which it was fashioned," and the soul to be "translated to that place where it shall take its abode until the final Resurrec-

---

11. For this point, I owe a debt of gratitude to William F. May's essay "The Sacral Power of Death in Contemporary Experience," in *On Moral Medicine: Theological Perspectives in Medical Ethics,* ed. Stephen E. Lammers and Allen Verhey (Grand Rapids: William B. Eerdmans, 1987), especially pp. 181-82.

12. *Rituale Armenorum: The Administration of the Sacraments and Breviary Rites of the Armenian Church,* ed. F. C. Conybeare (Oxford: Clarendon Press, 1905), p. 130. Gregory of Nyssa says the same: "Divine providence introduced death into human nature with a specific design so that by the dissolution of body and soul, vice may be drawn off and man may be refashioned again through the resurrection" (quoted by Florovsky in *Creation and Redemption,* p. 108).

tion."[13] Orthodox Christians pray for this dissolution not because they believe that death is good or out of despair but because they set their sights past death to the hope and promise of resurrection.

Spiritual Death

Corruptible death lies beyond the scope of physical, biological, or psychological science because in origin and end it transcends space and temporality, that which is physical and that which is psychological. Human sickness and death are also spiritual and eschatological. The medical notion of a precise moment of death measured in terms of cessation of brain function or the "closing down" of the body's system of vital organs is clinically useful, but it scarcely captures the complete reality or meaning of death. The demise of the biological individual is only a portion of death. Alexander Schmemann explained: "In the Christian vision, death is above all a *spiritual reality* of which one can partake while being alive, from which one can be free while lying in the grave. Death here is man's *separation from life*, and this means from God who is the only Giver of life."[14] Such a death may be a part of living: it does not belong exclusively to the biological demise of a person. The Christian vision of death encompasses scientific definitions of death as the terminus of biological life, but it also embraces spiritual and eschatological dimensions of human personhood. God, not nothingness, is the beginning, ground, and "end point" of all persons. Thus, contrary to modern perceptions and secular beliefs, human death is not the opposite of immortality. We

13. *Service Book of the Holy Orthodox–Catholic Apostolic Church,* ed. and trans. Isabel Florence Hapgood (Englewood, N.J.: Antiochian Orthodox Christian Archdiocese, 1975), p. 366.

14. Schmemann, *Of Water and the Spirit* (Crestwood, N.Y.: St. Vladimir's Seminary Press, 1974), p. 62.

THE VISION OF DEATH

come from God and are bound to return to God. But even if unrepentance obstructs our way back to God, our fate is not nothingness. God is Lord of both life and death, and death leads either to an unceasing separation from God and from the fellowship of the saints (Luke 16:19-31) or to a union in the company of the Holy Trinity of Father, Son, and Spirit. Sadly, many modern Christians seem to have lost hold of this vision of death and its place in God's salvation plan.

The Journey through Death

The great prayer attributed to St. Basil in the Armenian rite of burial reveals its vision of death in a sweeping narrative that explores the spiritual and eschatological dimensions of death I have just touched on and asks God to grant to the deceased person "a goodly journey" back to the Garden and the Tree of Life.

> We thank thee, Father of our Lord Jesus Christ, who because of thy love of mankind has visited us, and saved [us] from the machinations of the traducer [of] the race of men that were driven out and banished afar. For Satan was jealous of us, and drove us out of eternal life by his deceits and wiles, proscribing and banishing us unto our destruction and ruin. But thou, O God, who art benevolent and lovest mankind, didst not permit the bitterness of his poisoned fangs to remain in us. Wherefore thou didst summon death, and poured it out upon creatures, in order that the wickedness that had befallen might not remain immortal: but by removing us from this life, and cutting us from our sins, the punishment of the beneficent One became salvation.
>
> But in the last of days thou didst send thy only-begotten Son, beloved in the image of the death of sin; and he condemned sin in his own body, and by his voluntary crucifixion shattered the

hosts of the enemy. He became the firstfruits of them that slept, and by his divinely marvelous resurrection he invited us to share in his own immortality.

Now this thy servant believing in him has been baptized into the death of thy Christ. . . . Remit to this man his debts incurred either willingly or unwillingly, and heal all the wounds which the disincarnate enemy hath inflicted. . . .

And . . . heal his wounds, and convey him peacefully past the principalities of darkness. . . . And efface the handwriting of their influences and inworkings, which they have sown in him and vouchsafe to him a goodly journey. Let there be held far away from him and stayed the flaming sword, with which they guard the path of the Tree of life. . . . Let him through the same [so that he may] arrive at the place of safety where all thy saints are massed and wait for the great wedding, when the great God and Savior shall appear, Jesus Christ, at the sound of the great trumpet. . . . Then . . . at the glance of the judge the earth shall be shaken, and the sealed sepulchers be opened. The bodies that were turned to dust are built up afresh, and the spirits swooping down like eagles reach them and array themselves in the incorruptible body.[15]

The *Teaching of Saint Gregory* also employs this journey motif as it looks back to the exile from the Garden and looks forward to a return to it. God barred Adam and Eve from "the road to the tree of life," but from the very beginning God also anticipated their return: "For when he [each human being] is in the midst of the bitter taste and uncertainty of death, there will gradually come to his mind the memory of the tree, and with groaning he will seek approach to the garden of delight."[16] The prayer also projects the

15. *Rituale Armenorum*, pp. 130-31.
16. *The Teaching of Saint Gregory*, p. 52.

last stages of the journey through death back to the Garden. The dead will return to "the path of the Tree of Life" so that they might "arrive at the place of safety where all the saints are massed and wait the great wedding, when the great God and Savior shall appear, Jesus Christ."

In this tradition, death in Jesus Christ is a spiral that breaks free from the natural cycle of birth, death, and rebirth.[17] The lowest point of the spiral is death. But then the line curves upward beyond earthly life into eternal life. Christ gave death this upward curve by recapitulating our living and dying and then adding something else — a new creation. St. Paul describes it as the fruit of planting:

> But someone will ask, "How are the dead raised? With what kind of body do they come?" Fool! What you sow does not come to life unless it dies. And as for what you sow, you do not sow the body that is to be, but a bare seed. . . . God gives it a body as he has chosen. . . . So it is with the resurrection of the dead. What is sown is perishable, what is raised is imperishable. It is sown in dishonor, it is raised in glory. It is sown in weakness, it is raised in power. It is sown a physical body, it is raised a spiritual body. (1 Cor. 15:35-38, 42-44)

This sheds important light on the meaning of the Easter proclamation that death has been overcome once and for all in Christ Jesus. Christ abolished the corruptible form of death of which physical death is but a portion and a visible sign. The physical death that medicine knows, studies, and endeavors to delay is not the first issue here. God in Christ has taken the sting, the spiritual poison of sin, out of death through his own death so that our physical death becomes a sign of our destiny of communion with God.

17. I have drawn in this analysis from Jaroslav Pelikan's extraordinary little book *The Shape of Death* (Nashville: Abingdon Press, 1961), especially chap. 5.

Penance and the Reversal of Corruptible Death

The wounded surgeon plies the steel
That questions the distempered part;
Beneath the bleeding hands we feel
The sharp compassion of the healer's art
Resolving the enigma of the fever chart.

T. S. Eliot, "East Coker"

No description of the Christian vision of the origin, nature, and course of death is complete without the element of the doctrine and practice of penance. The first words of Jesus' teaching are: "Repent, for the kingdom of heaven has come near" (Matt. 4:17). Some have suggested that Jesus' command echoes God the Father's desire for repentance following Adam and Eve's decision to eat of the fruit of the Tree of Life. The Armenian *Teaching of Saint Gregory* speculates that immediately after they ate the forbidden fruit, God gave Adam and Eve one last opportunity to repent and to reverse the course of corruptible death. A key biblical passage is Genesis 3:9-10: "But the LORD God called to the man, and said to him, 'Where are you?' He said, 'I heard the sound of you in the garden, and I was afraid, because I was naked; and I hid myself.'" The *Teaching* interprets this passage to mean that "[God] wished by being somewhat indulgent to capture him [Adam], that the gentleness of God might lead them to penitence." Instead, the couple made excuses for themselves. "Then he [God] set judgment, passed sentence, which they paid and returned to dust [Gen. 3:19]; for the judgment of God is true over those who work evil."[18] One can see how the author of this catechism might have arrived at this speculation, for the Genesis story indicates that God expels the first couple from the Garden and from proximity to the Tree of Life only after he speaks to them

---

18. *The Teaching of Saint Gregory,* pp. 51-52.

this last time. And only then does Adam blame Eve for what he has done and Eve blame the serpent for what she has done (Gen. 3:12-13) — excuses and deceptions that seal God's judgment and invite corruptible death.

Since that point, say our sources, repentance alone has not been sufficient to reverse the process of corruptible death. St. Athanasius reasoned as follows: "Had it been a case of trespass only, and not of subsequent corruption, repentance would have been well enough; but when once transgression had begun men came under the power of corruption proper to their nature and were bereft of the grace which belonged to them as creatures in the Image of God."[19] The *Teaching of Saint Gregory* concludes, "For which reason, the God-seeing, holy prophets took care, like wise doctors [of faith], to prepare the medicine of cure for the pain of the illness, to remove and extirpate the scandal [of death] and destroy it completely."[20] As Eliot's poetry notes so profoundly, the last prophet and true doctor is Christ, who cured our sickness unto death, defeating death itself by his own righteous sacrifice on the cross.

Repentance and Healing

Death remains the outworking of sin in the human being, but it has also been transformed by Christ into the revelation of true life. In the Old Testament, the Hebrew word for "salvation" derives from *yasha,* which means "to save from a danger." God delivers us not only from our enemies and from persecution but also from sickness and from death itself. In the New Testament, the Greek *sozo* comes from *saos,*

19. *St. Athanasius on the Incarnation* (Crestwood, N.Y.: St. Vladimir's Seminary Press, 1982), p. 33.
20. *The Teaching of Saint Gregory,* p. 51.

meaning "healthy." Penance is for the sin that attaches to all "flesh" and makes this flesh subject to corruptible death; penance issues from the belief that God desires to heal our infirmities and make us whole.

The Orthodox sacraments of holy unction and burial amplify and deepen the meaning of this etymology of salvation. The Byzantine Rite of Holy Unction opens with a recitation of Psalms 143 and 51, which set the tone and direction of the entire rite.

> Hear my prayer, O LORD;
>> give ear to my supplications in your faithfulness;
>> answer me in your righteousness.
> Do not enter into judgment with your servant,
>> for no one living is righteous before you. . . .
>
> Answer me quickly, O LORD;
>> my spirit fails.
> Do not hide your face from me,
>> or I shall be like those who go down to the Pit.
> Let me hear of your steadfast love in the morning,
>> for in you I put my trust.
>
> (Psalm 143:1-2, 7-8)
>
> Have mercy on me, O God,
>> according to your steadfast love;
> according to your abundant mercy
>> blot out my transgressions.
> Wash me thoroughly from my iniquity,
>> and cleanse me from my sin.
>
> For I know my transgressions,
>> and my sin is ever before me.
> Against you, you alone, have I sinned,
>> and done what is evil in your sight,

THE VISION OF DEATH

so that you are justified in your sentence. . . .
Indeed, I was born guilty,
    a sinner when my mother conceived me.

You desire truth in the inward being;
    therefore teach me wisdom in my secret heart.
Purge me with hyssop, and I shall be clean; . . .
Let me hear joy and gladness;
    let the bones that you have crushed rejoice.
Hide your face from my sins,
    and blot out all my iniquities.

Create in me a clean heart, O God,
    and put a new and right spirit within me. . . .
Restore to me the joy of your salvation,
    and sustain in me a willing spirit.

                                (Psalm 51:1-10, 12)

The acts of repenting and asking God for forgiveness and healing are related to a profound understanding not only of death but of healing that encompasses the whole human being — spiritual and psychological as well as physical. In the Byzantine rite, a reading from the Epistle of James introduces this holistic interpretation of healing and sets the stage for anointing with oil:

Be patient, therefore, beloved, until the coming of the Lord. . . . As an example of suffering and patience, beloved, take the prophets who spoke in the name of the Lord. Indeed we call blessed those who showed endurance. You have heard of the endurance of Job, and you have seen the purpose of the Lord, how the Lord is compassionate and merciful. . . .

    Are any among you suffering? They should pray. Are any cheerful? They should sing songs of praise. Are any among you sick?

They should call the elders of the church and have them pray over them, anointing them with oil in the name of the Lord. The prayer of faith will save the sick, and the Lord will raise them up; and anyone who has committed sins will be forgiven. Therefore confess your sins to one another, and pray for one another, so that you may be healed. The prayer of the righteous is powerful and effective. (5:7, 10-11, 13-16)

Anointing with oil symbolizes the prayer, penance, forgiveness of sin, healing, and salvation that this passage mentions. Anointment indicates the deep connection between sickness and the mystery of God's redemptive purpose. It is not a substitute for medical care, but it reveals the telos of medicine nonetheless. The story of the Good Samaritan from the Gospel of Luke (10:25-38) introduces anointing, offering the assurance that even in the face of sickness and death God does not forget or abandon us, because his love is like that of the Samaritan, only stronger. Then a prefatory prayer reminds everyone present that God has made a lasting covenant with the Christian through baptism and chrismation and that God continues to honor this covenant as healer and redeemer in life and through death:

For thou art a great and marvelous God, who keepest thy covenant and thy mercy towards them that love thee; who givest remission of sins through thy Holy Child, Jesus; who regeneratest us from sin by Holy Baptism, and sanctifiest us with the Holy Spirit; who givest light to the blind, who raisest up them that are cast down, who lovest the righteous, and showest mercy unto sinners; who leadest us forth again out of darkness and the shadow of death.[21]

21. *Service Book of the Holy Orthodox–Catholic Apostolic Church*, p. 344.

A Tolstoyan Image of Penance

Tolstoy explores this deep signification of holy unction in his great short novel *The Death of Ivan Ilych*. Many Christian scholars have criticized Tolstoy for his advocacy of heterodox views in this novel and elsewhere in his fiction. Rather than stopping to assess this criticism, I want simply to propose an interpretation of this story that commends it as a forceful artistic exploration of the meanings of sin and death and penance and healing.

Most of the story consists of a retrospective description of the life that Ivan Ilych led until he was stricken by a mortal illness. This background shows us why Ivan's death is not merely physically painful but also spiritually and mentally agonizing. In the midst of dying, he discovers the court of his own conscience and comes to see himself guilty in the eyes of God. His understanding of his life is stripped of illusion and excuse. He is convicted of his pride and arrogance and the hollowness and superficiality of his relations with colleagues and family, and in the end he is led to repent.

Tolstoy masterfully draws his reader into the innermost thoughts and emotions of the dying man.

> His mental sufferings were due to the fact that at night, as he looked at [his servant] Gerasim's sleepy, good-natured face with its prominent cheek-bones, the question suddenly occurred to him: "What if my whole life has been wrong?" . . . And his professional duties, and the whole arrangement of his life and of his family, and all his social and official interests might all have been false. He tried to defend all those things to himself and suddenly felt the weakness of what he was defending. There was nothing to defend.[22]

22. Tolstoy, *The Death of Ivan Ilych,* in *Great Short Works of Leo Tolstoy,* trans. Louis Maude and Aylmer Maude (New York: Harper & Row, 1967), p. 299.

Ivan Ilych is moved by these shattering thoughts to take holy communion. Holy unction is not mentioned in the text, but Tolstoy's Russian readers would have assumed it as a matter of course, because in Orthodox practice communion is given in such circumstances only in conjunction with holy unction.[23] This unwritten subtext of the story is important, because it establishes the context of Ivan's subsequent thought and behavior. It clarifies the sequence of emotions that Ivan experiences: short-lived hope, crushing remorse and despair, and, finally, penance.

After the priest comes to hear his confession, Ivan feels "a relief from his doubts and consequently from his suffering, and for a moment there came a ray of hope. He again began to think of the vermiform appendix and the possibility of correcting it. He received the sacrament with tears in his eyes."[24]

At the outset Ivan naively expects that he will be miraculously cured. His disappointment when this does not happen and when, in fact, his condition further deteriorates is especially meaningful in the context of the sacrament of holy unction. The healing that God works in the penitent person transcends mere physical healing. God may or may not heal our physical infirmities, depending on the requirements of his unwavering greater purpose to redeem us for eternal life. The evil of corruptible death may be overcome even as a person's biological life draws to an end.

During the last three days of his life — three symbolic days of death and resurrection — Ivan Ilych perfects his last act, the act of

---

23. The association of holy unction with communion in this sort of context is evident in Tolstoy's account of the death of Nicholas Levin in *Anna Karenina:* "Next day the patient received Communion and Extreme Unction. During the ceremony he prayed fervently. In his large eyes, fixed upon an icon with a coloured cloth, was a look of such passionate entreaty and hope that Levin was frightened at seeing it. He knew that his passionate entreaty and hope would only make the parting from the life he so loved more difficult" (*Anna Karenina,* ed. George Gibian, trans. Louis Maude and Aylmer Maude [New York: W. W. Norton, 1970], p. 453).

24. Tolstoy, *The Death of Ivan Ilych,* p. 300.

dying, and his death is transformed into a redemptive event. Tolstoy's description is haunting.

> For three whole days, during which time did not exist for him, he struggled in that black sack into which he was being thrust by an invisible, restless force. . . . And every moment he felt despite all his efforts he was drawing nearer and nearer to what terrified him. He felt that his agony was due to his being thrust into that black hole, and still more his not being able to get into it. He was hindered from getting into it by his conviction that his life had been a good one. That very justification of his life held him fast and prevented his moving forward, and it caused him torment.[25]

This passage defines the crux of Ivan's penance and conversion.

Ivan's "conversion" follows the pattern of the dark night of the soul described by the Christian mystics and incorporated into Christian hagiography. This is the final surrender to death of the sinful self as repentance opens onto the ineffable divine light. The crucial moment of grace and forgiveness in the story is marked by the loving kiss and holy tears of Ivan's young son, which dissolve the last obstacle of pride that has prevented him from surrendering himself to God and his eternity.

> "Yes it [his life] was all not the right thing . . . but that's no matter. It can be done. But what is the right thing?" he asked himself, and suddenly grew quiet. This occurred at the end of the third day, two hours before his death. Just then his schoolboy son had crept softly in. . . . The dying man was still screaming desperately and waving his arms. His hand fell on the boy's head, and the boy caught it, pressed it to his lips, and began to cry. At that very

25. Tolstoy, *The Death of Ivan Ilych*, p. 301.

moment Ivan Ilych fell through and caught sight of the light, and it was revealed to him that though his life had not been what it should have been, this could still be rectified.[26]

Conclusion

We must all die; we are like water spilled on the ground, which cannot be gathered up. But God will not take away a life.

2 Samuel 14:14

In this discussion of *The Death of Ivan Ilych,* I have underlined and commended its redemptive vision. Yet there may be an even greater lesson to be learned, not from what the story says but from what it leaves unsaid. For I do not think that the pathos or tragedy of Ivan's life is wholly resolved by the ending that Tolstoy has supplied. What Ivan Ilych only begins to understand about living and dying at the end should ideally have been learned throughout the whole of his life. As I suggested in Chapter 2, remembrance of death is a virtue commended to Christians at their baptism and in all the sacraments. God calls every Christian to live toward dying by way of this mimesis and remembrance. Practicing this virtuous habit throughout life will prepare us for dying in a manner that preserves hope.

This wisdom is the core of Christian ethics of caring for the dying. It amounts to much more than the formal presentation of rules and principles of moral decision making that often count for what is called medical ethics and pastoral training in many professional schools and seminaries. A habit of affirming life in all circumstances without averting one's eyes from the awful reality of death belongs to a whole way of life, a faithful way of living toward

26. Tolstoy, *The Death of Ivan Ilych,* p. 301.

dying that all the Christian churches need to teach and cultivate. This fundamental instruction in Christian living toward dying is the necessary precondition for the ethic of caring for the dying that we will examine in the concluding chapters.

III

The Christian Ethics
of Caring for the Dying

4

The Case of Baby Rena: Cultural Confusions and Ethical Clarifications

THE Messiah, wrote Paul Ramsey, did not "bear epilepsy or psychosomatic disorders to gain victory over them in the flesh before the interventions of psychoneurosurgery. Rather is he said to have been born *mortal* flesh to gain for us a foretaste of victory over sin and death where those twin enemies had taken up apparently secure citadel."[1] The healing miracles performed by Jesus Christ, the Incarnate Son of God, are not merely metaphors or arbitrary signs for salvation. They are sacramental acts that bind together heaven and earth. All of Jesus' miraculous healings, and especially the raising of Lazarus, are signs and foreshadowings of his own victory over death on the cross.

As we have already noted, many in our culture are seeking to fabricate their own means to a victory over death. This is the essence of the thanatos syndrome and the vision of Dr. Jack Kevorkian. We see it in state initiatives to legalize physician-assisted suicide and in the rise of Derek Humphry's *Final Exit* to the best-seller lists. I

---

1. Ramsey, "The Indignity of 'Death and Dignity,'" in *On Moral Medicine: Theological Perspectives in Medical Ethics,* ed. Stephen E. Lammers and Allen Verhey (Grand Rapids: William B. Eerdmans, 1987), p. 192.

stated earlier that euthanasia is not the principal focus of this book, but I want nonetheless to take a brief look at it in preparation for a discussion of a specifically Christian ethic of caring for dying persons.

The God whose love is steadfast and whose mercy is abundant would never sanction euthanasia. However humanitarian or well-meaning the motives of those who advocate or practice euthanasia might be, they cannot justify what they do. In a Christian evaluation of the rightness or wrongness of euthanasia, the euthanizers' *aim* (i.e., their specific intent to bring about the death of an individual) is more important than their *motivation* (i.e., their desire to put an end to suffering). Or, to put it another way, the fact that euthanizers mean well is less important than the fact that the result of their "good intentions" is a person's death. While Christians might acknowledge the good intentions of those who in the name of humanitarianism practice euthanasia, we are constrained to condemn the act as sinful and wrong. The aim of euthanasia is contrary to everything God intends for us and has done for us in a fallen and sinful world, which, apart from his presence and saving activity, is a cosmic cemetery.[2]

There is a difference between a God-centered humanism and a naturalistic humanitarianism, and Christians must explain and emphasize that difference as a witness to an increasingly secular and utilitarian culture. To shed light on some of the important issues involved here, I want to take an extended look at the perplexing real-life case of a fourteen-month-old infant who died a painful and tragic death at a Washington, D.C., hospital.

2. See Gilbert C. Meilaender, "Euthanasia and Christian Vision," in *On Moral Medicine,* especially pp. 455-57.

The Case of Baby Rena

The story of how "Baby Rena" met her death was reported in a two-part front-page feature in the *Washington Post* in July of 1991.

> Murray Pollack, a physician at [Washington's] Children's Hospital, felt the time had come to change the rules. His 18-month old patient, Baby Rena, was dying, a victim of AIDS and heart disease. For six weeks, ever since her arrival at the intensive-care unit in late January, she had been breathing only with the help of a respirator. She was in so much pain that Pollack kept her constantly sedated. When nurses performed even the simplest procedure, such as weighing her, her blood pressure shot up and tears streamed down her face. But a tube in her throat made it impossible for her to utter a sound.[3]

Pollack had been called in to take the case after Baby Rena was brought to Children's Hospital on January 30. She died at the hospital on March 25. From the outset, Pollack judged that her case was probably "futile." In his view, keeping her on the respirator was not so much a life-saving measure as an intrusion into her dying process that intensified and prolonged her suffering. Pollack argued that he and the medical staff had "a responsibility to do what's best for Rena . . . , and to give her the appropriate care — and that is not always giving her all care."[4] Pollack was not advocating mercy killing. Rather, he wanted those responsible for her care to "let go" — to let Rena die the death she was dying as well as possible — and in his judgment that called for removing her from intensive

---

3. Benjamin Weiser, "A Question of Letting Go," *Washington Post*, 14 July 1991, p. 1.
4. Benjamin Weiser, "While Child Suffered, Beliefs Clashed," *Washington Post*, 15 July 1991, p. 6.

care and the respirator and providing medication to relieve her severe pain. Death would likely come sooner rather than later.

Children's Hospital requires the consent of parents or legal guardians to remove a minor from a respirator. Rena's mother had abandoned her at birth, making her a ward of the District government. She had been assigned foster parents, and while they had no legal standing in the decision, they strongly objected to Pollack's recommendations. They believed that God had told them "to take the child, and rear her in the nurture and admonition of God's word . . . and to battle the spirits of infirmity."[5] They demanded that her treatment "be motivated by a spiritual sense of obedience to God."[6] When the hospital sought the government's permission to take Rena off the respirator, the request was denied.

Baby Rena's foster parents, the pastor of their church, and their friends all played a significant role in determining the way in which she died. They all professed a Christian belief in the sanctity of life, and yet I cannot find a basis in my understanding of the Christian tradition to agree with either their reasoning or their judgment. Resources within the Christian faith lead me to believe that there are good reasons for drawing a distinction in health-care settings between directly killing people and allowing them to die. The former is euthanasia and is morally wrong; under certain circumstances, the latter is not. In fact, acquiescence in the face of an impending death may sometimes be required by Christian conscience. There are circumstances in which Christians are permitted — even duty bound — to let life ebb away in its natural course, so long as that course of action remains in accord with a corresponding duty to provide care that relieves pain and comforts the dying person.

Too often today, conscientious religious and nonreligious people alike lack the moral means to distinguish and accept such

5. Weiser, "A Question of Letting Go," p. 18.
6. Weiser, "While Child Suffered, Beliefs Clashed," p. 6.

possibilities. This issue, like so many other moral controversies, tends to get framed in either/or terms: either one believes that everything possible must be done to save life or one supports euthanasia. The Baby Rena case illustrates how people get caught up in this sort of moral cul-de-sac. Religious and nonreligious antagonists tend to view one another's arguments as proof positive that they are far apart in worldview, but in fact they often stand on common ground: both their positions are rooted in secularity.

In defending a distinction between direct killing (euthanasia) and allowing to die, Paul Ramsey once observed that people in our society who hold opposite positions on euthanasia often end up defining it in the same way. Religious conviction does not seem to be a determining factor.

> The case for either of these points of view [favoring euthanasia or favoring efforts to save life at all costs] can be made only by discounting and rejecting the arguments for saving life qualifiedly but not always. In both cases, an ethics of only caring for the dying is reduced to the moral equivalent of euthanasia — in the one case, to oppose this ever, in the other case, to endorse it. Thus, the extremes meet, both medical scrupulosity and euthanasia, in rejecting the discriminating concepts of traditional medicine.[7]

Operating on the basis of a simple definition of God's sovereignty over life and an almost Manichaean identification of sickness and death with the demonic spirits, Baby Rena's foster parents were incapable of making a distinction between euthanasia and caring for Rena to the point of letting her die. Ramsey insisted that the traditional ethic (grounded in the belief that God is Creator, Lord of Life, and Redeemer) clearly holds that "letting life ebb away

7. Ramsey, *The Patient as Person* (New Haven: Yale University Press, 1970), p. 146.

is *not* the same as actively encompassing a patient's life."[8] How is it that Baby Rena's foster parents, devoted religious people, failed to see and act on this important distinction? Why is it that they were held captive to the current popular meaning of euthanasia, to thinking in terms of the restrictive alternatives of either a utilitarian devaluation of life or an ethical vitalism that mystifies and absolutizes human life?

I think Alexander Schmemann had it basically right when he argued that the mark of secularism is the absence of God experienced in society and in people's lives. Vast numbers of people in our culture, religious and nonreligious alike, carry this mark of secularism in their understandings of God and the world, and this is nowhere more evident than in their attitudes toward death and dying.

Unconvinced of the existence of God or an afterlife, nonreligious secularists typically associate all value in life with human agency — human projects to eliminate suffering, injustice, and the like. They refuse to explain the world "in terms of an 'other world' of which no one knows anything, and life . . . in terms of a 'survival' about which no one has the slightest idea." Rejecting religious orthodoxies that ground the value of life in terms of death and an afterlife, they explain "death in terms of life."[9]

These nonreligious secularists may differ among themselves, however, about the scale of value on which human life ought to be measured. Some hold personal existence as the only concrete value and adhere to an ethical vitalism that insists on using every means possible in all circumstances to ward off personal death. Others reason from a utilitarian framework that the value of a life is qualified by the degree of good or happiness, pleasure or fulfillment that

8. Ramsey, *The Patient as Person*, p. 156.

9. Alexander Schmemann, *For the Life of the World: Sacraments and Orthodoxy* (Crestwood, N.Y.: St. Vladimir's Seminary Press, 1973), p. 98.

might reasonably be expected in it. On the basis of this quality-of-life principle, they argue that some lives might not be worth living, and hence that we might properly choose to end them through physician-assisted suicide or euthanasia.

Of late, increasing numbers of individuals are claiming the right and the competence to make such decisions.[10] In this regard, Dr. Jack Kevorkian is hardly exceptional. The medical ethicist Daniel Callahan has astutely pointed out the hubris of such claims and how they can lead to an outright denial of the distinction between killing and letting die. The argument for euthanasia and the legalization of physician-assisted suicide is basically "about the centrality and validity of control," says Callahan. "By making a denial of the distinction between killing and allowing to die central to the argument, the euthanasia movement has embodied the assumption, the conceit actually, that man is now wholly in control of everything, responsible for all life and all death."[11]

On the face of it, religious people like Baby Rena's foster parents who make the "other" spiritual world the measure of all value seem to be the opposite of nonreligious secularists. They profess to assign all ultimate decisions about life and death to God rather than human beings. And yet, significantly, both camps ground their reasoning in the presupposition that the world is essentially meaningless because God is absent from it. The nonreligious secularists simply remove God from the equation on the basis of either atheistic or agnostic presumptions; people like Baby Rena's foster parents — who I believe can be fairly characterized as religious

---

10. More than twenty years ago, Marya Mannes argued this way in *Last Rights* (New York: William Morrow, 1974). More recently, medical ethicist Margaret P. Battin has dismissed religious proscriptions of suicide and euthanasia and advocated a fundamental right of suicide (*Least Worst Death: Essays in Bioethics on the End of Life* [New York: Oxford University Press, 1994]).

11. Callahan, *What Kind of Life: The Limits of Medical Progress* (New York: Simon & Schuster, 1990), p. 242.

secularists — effectively act as though God is restricted to a spiritual realm and is wholly absent from this fallen and sin-ridden world. From the standpoint of the classical Christian understanding of life and death, both camps inappropriately devalue the world by presuming that God is absent from it. The nonreligious secularists look only to human endeavor for meaning and single-mindedly seek to alleviate human suffering by whatever means possible, including the facilitation of death. The religious secularists look only to the spiritual realm for meaning and single-mindedly seek to preserve human life at all costs, on the grounds that such life is a gift from God that ought to be sustained at all costs, no matter what amount of physical suffering might be involved in the process of dying.

I believe that Baby Rena's foster parents made their decisions about her welfare on the basis of this kind of secular religious worldview. Their own description of their beliefs suggests that their religion is rooted in a metaphysical and moral dualism that radically separates physical existence (this world) from spiritual existence (the other world). This body-and-spirit dualism moved otherwise loving adults to insist that a small child's extreme physical pain be prolonged.

But what does it mean to care for the spiritual well-being of a loved one who is dying if that care does not include seriously taking account of the physical pain she endures and the imminence of her death?[12] During one conversation between the hospital staff

12. Kathleen M. Foley, a physician and professor at the Memorial Sloan-Kettering Cancer Center, has written extensively on the all-too-common failure to prescribe pain-reducing medicines and treatments to patients in advanced stages of cancer and other terminal illnesses. She argues that the growing interest in physician-assisted suicide might be more properly addressed if physicians and health-care providers were better educated in pain assessment and treatment and if patients and their families were better informed of their options. See, e.g., "The Relationship of Pain and Symptom Management to Patient Requests for Physician-Assisted Suicide," *Journal of Pain and Symptom Management,* 5 July 1991, pp. 289-97.

Baby Rena's foster parents stood in the way of reducing her pain, but it is even more often the case that attending physicians allow their patients to suffer needlessly because they are not sufficiently well trained in assessing pain and supplying reme-

and the parents, the foster father sketched three pictures, repre-
senting Rena's body, soul, and spirit. "We see that she has AIDS,"
he said. "It's real, because you can see it under the microscope." He
went on to thank the hospital staff for working hard to meet her
medical needs — the needs of her body. But he complained that
they were ignoring her spiritual side. Pointing to the third sketch,
he said, "It seems to me that until the hospital really addresses the
spiritual area we won't be able to defeat these various spirits of

---

dies. This judgment is supported by a recently published five-year study, the largest
of its kind, which included the responses of over nine thousand patients in five teaching
hospitals. The study was designed "to improve end-of-life decision making and reduce
the frequency of a mechanically supported, painful, and prolonged death." The results
were disappointing. "The phase I observation confirmed substantial shortcomings in
care of seriously ill hospitalized adults. The phase II intervention failed to improve
care or patient outcomes. Enhancing opportunities for more patient-physician communication, although advocated as the major method for improving outcomes," was
found to be "inadequate to change established practices" ("A Controlled Trial to
Improve Care for Seriously Ill Hospitalized Patients," *Journal of the American Medical
Association* 274 [22/29 November 1995]: 1591). The report concluded, "We are left
with a troubling situation. The picture we describe of the care of seriously ill or dying
persons is not attractive. One would certainly prefer to envision that, when confronted
with life-threatening illnesses, the patient and family would be included in discussions,
realistic estimates of outcome would be valued, pain would be treated, and dying
would not be prolonged. That is still a worthy vision" (p. 1597).

The *Washington Post* cited Joanne Lynn, the director of the Center to Improve
Care of the Dying at George Washington University Medical Center as saying that
"she was dumbfounded by the finding that more than one-third of the patients [in
the study] died in pain. 'We would never tolerate rates like this for post-operative
infections.'" In fact, the study revealed that "more than half of the patients who died
were reported by their families in moderate or severe pain during most of their final
three days of life." This figure is even more staggering given that the subjects of the
report were a controlled group of patients who were supposed to benefit from the
initiatives implemented by the study. The report stated that the most disturbing finding
was that the measures that were meant "to improve care failed to have any discernible
impact" (Don Colburn, *Washington Post,* 22 November 1995, p. 10).

I believe that to some extent it was inevitable that this study would be disappointing. The crisis in the ethos of medicine and medical care runs so deep that it
cannot be resolved by procedure alone.

infirmity, including AIDS, that we're fighting against here." He explained his belief that the decisions about Rena needed "to be motivated by a spiritual sense of obedience to God. It's most important to find out what God desires or what God wills for Rena." At one point, a hospital social worker said, "What you're saying is that you don't want to give up on the spiritual part even though we're giving up on the physical part." The father nodded his head. He recalled an earlier occasion on which Rena had rallied after the hospital staff had given up hope. "If we give up now, we won't fully understand. . . . We won't fully know that God's word is true."[13]

The foster father spoke of the need to discover what God wants as if that wasn't already evident at the level of Baby Rena's fleshly suffering and dying. What more could the parents possibly have been waiting for to reveal God's will in the situation? As Ramsey so aptly put it, "No Biblical theologian should take umbrage at the suggestion that a pronouncement of death is a medical question." Indeed, I would broaden that to say that no Christian should take umbrage at the suggestion that judgments about when death is imminent or further medical treatment is futile are properly medical determinations. "What personal life do we know except within the ambiance of a bodily existence?"[14] God does not need respirators to work miracles, but God entrusts determinations of whether we are biologically dying to our physicians whether they themselves trust in him or not. One writer of a letter to the editors of the *Washington Post* questioned the foster parents' identification of the will of God with doing everything possible to keep Rena alive:

> I hope that people reading the article on Baby Rena do not get the impression that keeping her on the respirator was the only decision that people with faith in God could have made. . . .

13. Weiser, "While Child Suffered, Beliefs Clashed," p. 6.
14. Ramsey, *The Patient as Person,* p. 61.

Having faith [sometimes] requires people to voluntarily give control over a situation to God. Although giving up control is the key to doing God's will, you still need to figure out what it is that God wants you to do — that's the hard part.[15]

Preserving the Moral Distinction between Killing and "Letting Die"

In his remarkable little book *The Patient as Person*, Paul Ramsey ruminates,

It may be that only in an age of faith when men know that dying cannot pass beyond God's love and care will men have the courage to apply limits [to lifesaving interventions in] medical practice. It may be that only upon the basis of faith in God can there be a conscionable category of "ceasing to oppose death," making room for caring for the dying. It may also be that only an age of faith is productive of absolute limits upon the taking of the lives of terminal patients, because of the alignment of many a human will with God's care for them here and now, and not only in the there and then of his providence.[16]

Baby Rena's foster parents were far more fixed on the "there and then" of God's providence than on any sort of effort to discern the alignment of the many human wills involved in her care with God's care. As I have been suggesting, this fixation on the "there and then" and a corresponding devaluation of the "here and now" belongs to

15. "The Agonizing Decisions Surrounding Baby Rena" (letter from Monica Michelizzi), *Washington Post*, 22 July 1991, p. 10.
16. Ramsey, *The Patient as Person*, p. 156.

a spiritualism and otherworldliness that are the symptom and product of secularism itself, not its opposite, as those who hold such religious views typically think. This is one area in which there is no practical difference between a secularized Christianity and modern fundamentalism. Nonreligious secularism is characteristically expressed in a desacralization of human life and the experienced world; Judeo-Christian religious secularism is characteristically expressed in the breakdown of the symbolic and sacramental structures in and by which individuals and communities experience God as both transcendent over the world and wholly manifest within it. Baby Rena's foster parents made repeated appeals to God and his law, but they were unable to imagine that God's encompassing love might permit a practical ethical distinction in the "here and now" between direct killing and letting die. They could not imagine that a merciful God would sanction allowing Baby Rena to die. The Orthodox Christian tradition, on the other hand, views this sort of allowing to die as not merely permissible but actually desirable in some cases, as we noted in Chapter 3 in our consideration of the prayer for the hastening of the dying process.

The articles in the *Washington Post* did not say whether Dr. Pollack was a religious man, but when I compare his proposals for Baby Rena's medical care with those of her foster parents, I believe that his proposals were more in keeping with the classical Christian conviction that in the here and now God's care should be aligned with human reason and judgment in decisions about when life is ebbing and need not be heroically extended. In making this judgment, I am simply comparing Pollack's plea that Baby Rena be allowed to die with the foster parents' insistence that her life be prolonged at all costs; I am not unqualifiedly endorsing Pollack's ethical reasoning, because I can't know fully what that reasoning entailed. The newspaper reports suggest that Pollack based his ethical judgment on a medical determination of the futility of additional treatment and a concern for the quality of the patient's remaining life. But there is nothing in the newspaper's description of Pollack's reasoning to indicate that he never considered euthanasia a possible solution to Baby Rena's plight or that it would have violated his ethical standards to have proposed such a course of action. For Christians, the distinction between killing and letting die is key.

Daniel Callahan provides a definition that is helpful in our efforts to make this distinction:

"Letting die" is only possible if there is some underlying disease that will serve as the cause of death. Put me on a respirator now, when I am in good health, and nothing whatever will happen if it is turned off. I cannot be "allowed to die" by having a respirator turned off if I have healthy lungs. It is wholly different, however, if a doctor gives me a muscle-relaxing injection that will paralyze my lungs. Healthy or not, those lungs will cease to function and I will die. That is what it means to "kill" someone as distinguished from "letting" someone die. Put more formally, there must be an underlying fatal pathology if allowing to die is even possible. Killing, by contrast, provides its own fatal pathology. Nothing but the action of the doctor giving the lethal injection is necessary to bring about death.[17]

It has been argued that one need not appeal to faith in God to secure this distinction within medical ethics. This is essentially Callahan's own position.[18] But on this point I side with Ramsey. In the relatively rarefied atmosphere of medical ethics, it may be possible to establish principles and rules that secure a distinction between killing and letting die without recourse to the resources of

17. Callahan, *The Troubled Dream of Life* (New York: Simon & Schuster, 1993), p. 77.
18. Callahan establishes this position in both *What Kind of Life* and *The Troubled Dream of Life*. See also chap. 2 of James F. Childress's *Priorities in Medical Ethics* (Philadelphia: Westminster Press, 1981).

the Christian tradition. But, as Ramsey suggests, it is becoming increasingly difficult to maintain this distinction as the moral force of biblical theism diminishes in our culture. Biblically rooted theism provides us with the conviction that God, the absolute source and sustainer of our being and our Redeemer, does not abandon us in death. As St. Paul says, "Neither death, nor life, . . . nor anything else in all creation, will be able to separate us from the love of God" (Rom. 8:38-39). Biblical theism has a vision of a *summum bonum* that supports making calibrated judgments about the kind and extent of the care we owe to those who are in the last stages of dying. But this vision is not predominant in our culture. The distinction between killing and letting die is not anchored in anything; not even appeals to the principle of trust between patient and physician or the doctor's Hippocratic oath seem sufficient.

We can find evidence of this problem in one of John Updike's short stories entitled "Killing." As the story opens, a young woman named Anne is sitting with her dying father in a nursing home. A series of strokes has left him unconscious, unable to swallow or communicate. Anne has made the decision that he should be kept in the nursing home rather than moved to a hospital where he would be fed intravenously. The hospital treatment might be able to extend his life, but it would not be able to change the fact that his condition is hopeless. Wherever he will lie, death will be near at hand. The attending physician has assured Anne that she has acted wisely, but she remains plagued with guilt. She cannot shake the thought that by leaving her father in the nursing home she has in effect ordered his execution. As Updike puts it, she "realized that her decision had been to kill her father. He could not swallow. He could not drink. Abandoned he must die."[19]

19. Updike, "Killing," in *Trust Me* (New York: Fawcett Crest, 1987), p. 16. Updike describes the dying man as having parched lips and as exuding a putrid stench from his mouth. This is a realistic description of a patient who fails to receive the proper care in such a situation. To prevent dehydration and discomfort, caregivers

Most medical ethicists agree that in certain terminal cases, when intravenous feeding might actually contribute to pain or discomfort and needlessly slow the inevitable dying process, a decision like the one Anne authorizes is morally permissible.[20] But no one seems to have communicated this to Anne. She seems to be ignorant of the medical-ethical distinction between killing and letting die. There is no indication that she has been told why withholding intravenous feeding might be appropriate in her father's case. In the end, however, it is not really likely that such information and counseling would suffice to allay Anne's anguish. Denied essential supportive relationships, she is lacerated by her conflicting love for and revulsion at her bedridden, dying father. Like so many of her contemporaries, she has been cast into a situation for which she is ill prepared. While her sentiments run deep, her moral resources are threadbare and poorly defined. And, as is the case with so many other women in our society (in which this burden more often than not falls on women), she is alone in the time of crisis. She has been abandoned by an estranged husband, and her siblings are too busy and too distant to bother to help. Nor does she have a religious community in which she might voice her feelings of guilt and find forgiveness.

In "Killing," Updike ruthlessly unmasks the desolation of modern life that we try to cover with technology, therapeutic strategies, and euphemism. More important, through the compelling character of Anne he shows us how family members who are forced to make decisions about dying loved ones are often pushed to the precipice of total despair and an exhausted embrace of the thanatos syndrome. In Anne's case, an "irrational" love for father, a lingering legacy of

must provide a regimen of oral hygiene and topical application of wetting agents or sipping fluids if the patient is conscious (see Joyce V. Zerwekh, "The Dehydration Question," *Nursing,* January 1983, pp. 47-51).

20. See Bonnie Steinbock, Joanne Lynn, James Childress, and Daniel Callahan, "Feeding the Dying Patient," *Hastings Center Report,* 5 October 1983, pp. 13-22.

guilt from a largely moribund Christian past, and the unavailability of legal physician-assisted suicide or euthanasia combine to lead her to an otherwise reasonable and probably right decision. But one has to wonder how soon her character will be superseded in our literature by a "compassionate" and "heroic" daughter who has no qualms about authorizing euthanasia for her dying father.

Conclusion

In light of the tragic story of Baby Rena, there is one practical point that I would like to stress: biblical faith does make it possible for us to make reasonable moral judgments about when our primary obligation to a patient is not to do everything possible to extend her life but rather to care for her as if she is dying. There can come a time when we should no longer seek to cure the patient but should instead turn our efforts to providing care for her in order that her death be the best possible death. Informed by a true biblical faith, we will seek to navigate a course between an absolutistic ethical vitalism on the one hand and a utilitarian ethic of "quality of life," triage, and euthanasia on the other. In the concluding chapter we will turn to an exploration of some of the finer points of a biblically informed ethic of caring for the dying.

5

Caring for the Dying
in the Christian Faith

They are and suffer; that is all they do;
A bandage hides the place where each is living,
his knowledge of the world restricted to
The treatments that the instruments are giving

And lie apart like epochs from each other
— Truth in their sense is how much they can bear;
It is not like ours, but groans they smother —
And are remote as plants; we stand elsewhere.

For who when healthy can become a foot?
Even a scratch we can't recall when cured,
But are boist'rous in a moment and believe

In the common world of the uninjured, and cannot
Imagine isolation. Only happiness is shared,
And anger, and the idea of love.

W. H. Auden, "Surgical Ward"

As WE HAVE already noted, modern people tend to have both an aversion to death and an obsession with it. These appositional responses to death are mirrored in contemporary health care and policy debate. As Paul Ramsey notes, "A culture that defines death as always a disaster will be one that is tempted to resolve these questions in terms of triage — disaster medicine."[1] So it is that the thanatos syndrome has begun to permeate our society's ethos in medicine and health care.

Early in the public debate over the ill-fated Clinton plan for a national health-care system, a proposal was floated in the press that would have caught Ramsey's attention. It suggested that people over a given age be ineligible for certain costly medical treatments — treatments that in principle are available to all Americans today regardless of age. There is a growing consensus that burgeoning case loads, limited resources, and escalating costs are going to demand more rationing of medical resources in certain places and for certain treatments. Many people remain troubled by the prospect, although they might be inclined to view the rationing of treatment for terminally ill or dying persons as ethically justifiable if such rationing were carefully circumscribed and limited to the very worst cases — that is to say, so long as the vast majority of the terminally ill were cared for in the very best way possible. Rationing of this sort would at least preserve and honor a cardinal principle of Western ethics — namely, the fundamental equality of all human beings. The proposal to ration care on the basis of age, on the other hand, was based on a baldly utilitarian ethic of cost effectiveness backed up with endless batteries of survivability statistics. In a utilitarian climate, these statistics can overwhelm the moral principles that secure the true value of human life and set firm limits to what we ought and ought not do in such life-and-death situations.

1. Ramsey, *The Patient as Person* (New Haven: Yale University Press, 1970), p. 118.

A spurt of recent lower-court rulings that rely heavily on such statistical information and appeal strongly to utilitarian quality-of-life arguments may be ominous indicators of where our society is headed. These court decisions could be opening the door to broader legal acceptance of arguments that the lives of some people are worth less than others — that lives of the elderly, say, are worth less than those of individuals in the prime of life. If these arguments from utility and quality of life gain acceptance in the culture at large, we will inevitably move away from a traditional medicine centered on patient treatment toward a "public policy" medicine based in triage and rationing. The old ethical personalism will be replaced by a quality-of-life standard that in coldly utilitarian fashion reduces individuals to statistical profiles.

In the pages that follow I am not going to try to work through all of the practical dimensions of this or other aspects of the ongoing public policy debate. My goal is at once more theological and more immediate. I want to focus on Christian practices rooted in the two central theological principles introduced in Chapter 3 — first, that sin and death are mystically related, and second, that healing and salvation are intimately connected. The Christian practice that corresponds to the first theological principle is *penance*. The practice corresponding to the second theological principle, premised in the salvific effects of the Incarnation, is what I will be calling *suffering under the sign of the cross*. The practices of penance and suffering under the sign of the cross produce forgiveness, reconciliation, and spiritual healing. Each practice has an important role to fill in the context of the church's prayer, sacraments, and pastoral care.

Penance and Forgiveness in Caring for the Dying

*True contrition is not merely sorrow over our failures, for
that would but emphasize the gaps. It is not merely the resolve
to do better next time which leaves the past as it was. The
contrite man returns to the past act and enters into it until
he knows and judges it with reason, his will, his intention,
and does so in the face of the living, holy God.*

Romano Guardini, *The Last Things*

There are bound to be objections in a therapeutic and utilitarian
climate to the exceptional attention that is given to sin and
penance in many Christian rites. Secular ethicists and medical
practitioners will charge that references to sin and penance are
insensitive and inappropriate in a program of care for terminally
ill or dying patients. I am quite willing to concede that these
themes are subject to abuse by religious people in pastoral and
health-care professions. Condescension and punitive impulses can
turn what is supposed to be healing into another form of torment
for the afflicted.[2] There are among the clergy and laity of every
church contemporary counterparts of Job's so-called friends who
are motivated by an inflexible orthodoxy or other reasons to
assume the divine prerogative of judgment and who add to the
suffering of countless afflicted by reminding them incessantly of
their sins and failures.

But these abuses of a penitential theology do not discredit the
profound and practical wisdom of the church when it places repentance and forgiveness at the center of its ministry to the sick

2. For a discussion of this, see William F. May, "The Sacral Power of Death in
Contemporary Experience," in *On Moral Medicine: Theological Perspectives in Medical
Ethics,* ed. Stephen E. Lammers and Allen Verhey (Grand Rapids: William B. Eerd-
mans, 1987), p. 181.

and dying. This emphasis makes perfect sense in the light of the Gospels and indeed the whole of Scripture. The Orthodox rites wisely take account of the burden of personal guilt that frequently weighs heavily on the mind of a sick or dying person. In such circumstances, the mistakes that a person has made or the wrongs and injustices he has committed over a lifetime can suddenly return to haunt him in devastating ways. These circumstances may deeply and existentially confound what meaning a person has made of his life.

We have already reflected on the painful journey of Tolstoy's Ivan Ilych through regret for his life of sin and considered the ways in which the rite of holy unction serves to facilitate the process of resolving such guilt, especially through repentance and reconciliation. The Byzantine Rite of Holy Unction contains several psalms and prayers that invite sick persons to review their lives penitently. Among the prayers is the following:

> We thank thee, O Lord our God, who art good and lovest mankind, the Physician of our souls and bodies, who painlessly has borne our iniquities, by whose stripes we have been healed. . . . We beseech thee . . . in thy goodness loose, remit, forgive, O God, the errors of thy servant, and his (her) iniquities. . . . Whether through the sight of his (her) eyes, or his (her) sense of smell, whether through the union of adultery or the taste of fornication, or through whatever impulse of the flesh and of the spirit he (she) hath departed from thy will, and from thy holiness. . . . For thou art our God, who hast given us a commandment by thy holy Apostles, saying: Whatsoever ye bind on earth shall be bound in heaven, and whatsoever ye loose on earth shall be loosed in heaven. And again: Unto whomsoever ye remit sins, unto him they shall be remitted, and if ye retain them, they shall be retained. And as thou didst hearken unto Ezekiel in the sorrow of his soul, at the hour of his death, and didst not despise his supplications, so also,

in like manner, give ear unto me, thy humble, and sinful, and unworthy servant at this hour.[3]

This prayer recalls and invokes repentance and divine judgment and forgiveness, and it provides heuristic insight into Ivan's suffering and conversion at the end of the story. Why does Ivan suffer so much more from mental anguish and guilt than from physical pain? His Russian and Orthodox identity is one important key to answering that question. The prayer just cited, for example, also recalls great sinners of the Bible who were forgiven by God or were accepted by Christ because they repented: "We thank thee, O Lord our God, who art good and lovest mankind, the Physician of our souls and bodies, . . . who didst justify the Publican by thy word, and didst accept the Thief at his last confession; who takest away the sins of the world, and wast nailed to the Cross."[4] This kind of prayer and expression of Orthodox piety both accuses and comforts Ivan's conscience. An integral part of his cultural environment, it helps to explain his behavior and thoughts in the closing scene when he is joined at bedside by family members. Ivan struggles to ask for forgiveness but is so weak that he is unable to utter the words: "He tried to add 'Forgive me,' but said 'Forego' and waved his hand, knowing that He whose understanding mattered would understand."[5]

Yet another prayer in the rite declares that by baptism God has inscribed us with "the image of his Cross" through anointing "by holy Oil."[6] We gain insight into Tolstoy's vivid and moving

3. *Service Book of the Holy Orthodox–Catholic Apostolic Church*, ed. and trans. Isabel Florence Hapgood (Englewood, N.J.: Antiochian Orthodox Christian Archdiocese, 1974), p. 355.

4. *Service Book of the Holy Orthodox–Catholic Apostolic Church*, p. 355. Aside from the "Our Father," the prayer of the publican and the words of the thief on the cross are the most repeated biblical prayers in Orthodox liturgy.

5. Tolstoy, *The Death of Ivan Ilych*, in *Great Short Works of Leo Tolstoy*, trans. Louis Maude and Aylmer Maude (New York: Harper & Row, 1967), p. 302.

6. *Service Book of the Holy Orthodox–Catholic Apostolic Church*, p. 344.

description of Ivan's very last moments: "'It is finished!', someone said. He [Ivan] heard these words and repeated them in his soul. 'Death is finished,' he said to himself. 'It is no more!' He drew in a breath, stopped in the midst of a sigh, stretched out, and died."[7]

In this great story, an unattractive character is given the opportunity to repent and experiences genuine forgiveness and reconciliation before he dies. Sr. Sharon M. Burns, a theologian and the chaplain at the Stella Maris Hospice in Towson, Maryland, argues that "reconciliation is the most crucial thing for the dying irrespective of whether or not the person is religious or secular." This being the case, the staff at Stella Maris are frustrated when doctors hold off sending dying patients to them until the last minute. Burns stresses the difference between curing and healing, noting that a person can be healed even as he is dying. "Even as their bodies are disintegrating they are becoming whole."[8]

Forgiveness and reconciliation are crucial for this healing process — both reconciliation with others and reconciliation with one's own past. Simply telling people that "they are forgiven by a good and loving God often is not sufficient," says Sr. Burns. "They need to acknowledge their guilt . . . , to ask for forgiveness (sometimes directly of the person whom they have hurt), and to forgive themselves."[9] The Armenian Rite for Communion of the Sick is an occasion for just this sort of reconciliation and forgiveness. It clarifies the Christian wisdom that belongs to Tolstoy's story and that Sr. Burns commends from her pastoral experience. The rubrics indicate that the priest shall take "the saving mystery and the cross and censor . . . , and go to the sick man. . . . But it is *fitting* that the sick man should first hold converse with his intimate friends or with

7. Tolstoy, *The Death of Ivan Ilych*, p. 302.
8. Burns, in an interview with the author conducted in June of 1993.
9. Burns, "The Spirituality of Dying," *Health Progress*, September 1991, p. 50.

any one else with all vigilance and circumspection. And if he has any grudge against anyone, he shall forgive him."[10]

Forgiveness and Reconciliation within the Community of the Faithful

There is another aspect of the practice of penance in the Orthodox tradition that we should consider at this juncture: the social dimension of penance. As we have already noted, the Bible and Orthodox tradition teach that sickness is often enmeshed consciously and unconsciously in the complexities of personal and collective sin. Sometimes there is a clear connection between individual sins (and bad habits) and sickness. In such cases, it may be appropriate for pastors to remind their parishioners of the link between their behavior and their sickness.

This is not to say that we should casually equate sickness with punishment for sins, however. Jesus repudiates this inference (Luke 13:3-4). Nevertheless, a deep interior connection of sin to sickness and death remains. Orthodox Christian penance encompasses not only personal but also social dimensions of sin as the church seeks to strengthen the bonds of communal love and concern that can provide hope and encouragement to sick people. Recent studies have begun to confirm that people whose community and family life are strong experience pain less frequently and less intensely than people whose community and family life are breaking down.

Presently, all of the Christian churches are affected by a shift from a historical emphasis on penance and communal responsibility to modern self-affirmation and extreme individualism. Their need

10. *Rituale Armenorum: The Administration of the Sacraments and Breviary Rites of the Armenian Church,* ed. F. C. Conybeare (Oxford: Clarendon Press, 1905), pp. 114-15.

to recapture a deepened understanding of the social character of penance for a contemporary Christian ethic of caring for the dying is especially acute now because so many other communal links have broken down and disappeared in our culture. Fortunately, the resources with which to begin this retrieval of the wisdom about the social dimensions of sin, suffering, penance, and healing are readily at hand. We have already surveyed some of the ways in which the prayers in the Orthodox rites of holy unction place personal sin firmly within the social matrix of evil and suffering. The supposition that individuals participate in Adam's sin and within a larger, encompassing mystical body of fallen, sinful humanity is the theological foundation of this practice. Personal sin begets corporate sin, and corporate sin begets personal sin. We pay the price in a broad spectrum of physical and psychological illnesses as well as mortality. The Orthodox rites are specifically constructed to break this vicious circle.

> Yea, O Lord who art easy to be entreated; who alone art merciful and lovest mankind, who repentest thee of our evil deeds; who knowest how the mind of man is applied unto wickedness, even from his youth up . . . and didst thyself become a created being for the sake of thy creatures; thou hast said: I am not come to call the righteous but sinners to repentance. . . . Thou didst not abhor the sinful woman who washed thy precious feet with her tears; thou didst say, There is joy in heaven over one sinner who repenteth. Do thou, O tender-hearted Master, look down from the height of thy sanctuary, overshadowing us sinners, who are also thine unworthy servants, with the grace of the Holy Spirit, at this hour, and take up thine abode in thy servant, _____, who acknowledgeth his (her) iniquities and draweth near unto thee in faith.[11]

11. *Service Book of the Holy Orthodox–Catholic Apostolic Church*, p. 347.

This prayer from the Byzantine Rite of Holy Unction draws attention not only to the sins of the sick person but also to the sins of the family and friends who gather at the bedside or in the church. This attention to corporate sin is important for a Christian ethic of caring for the dying, because it helps to take some of the weight of failure off the sick and preclude their alienation from the healthy. Even more important, the prayer reconstitutes the church as a community of penitent sinners aware of their common frailty and mortality who, in the words of the Armenian service for communion of the sick, look together to God "for wholeness of souls and bodies, . . . and for the perfection of good works and of all virtues."[12] The healthy are reminded that they are not so very different from the afflicted in their midst, and the afflicted are drawn back into the body that loves and forgives all of its members.

Penance and Life Review

Before leaving this discussion of penance, I want to consider what modern therapy calls "life review" — a practice endorsed by both psychologists and theologians that has the potential to enhance our understanding of how penance might be applied in new ways to care for the dying.

In reflecting on her experience as a hospice chaplain and spiritual counselor, Sr. Sharon Burns has observed that people who are gravely ill or dying often want to make an accounting of their lives — and that this can be a significant part of the healing process. She states that in order to heal spiritually,

People who are dying or have a life-threatening illness need help to reflect on this present moment of their lives. . . . Patients enter

12. *Rituale Armenorum*, p. 116.

hospice when nothing can be done to arrest their terminal illness. . . . Even though hospice personnel cannot hope for a cure,
they can see the possibility of *healing,* that is, the achievement of
spiritual unity that produces wholeness of being. . . . Efforts to
help patients toward wholeness necessitate helping them accept
freely their whole lives, all phases of their lives, past, present, and
future.[13]

In Iris Murdoch's novel *Nuns and Soldiers,* an atheist dying of
cancer confides in an estranged nun, "I wish I believed in a
hereafter. . . . Not for any vulgar reason of course. Not just to be
let off this thing that's happening in the next few weeks. But — it's
something I've always felt. . . . I would like to be judged."[14] The
gist of his desire is that he would like the assurance of having "a
clear account" of his life. He feels that his life should have some
consequences, even if they were to include punishment. But why
an afterlife, he is asked. "Oh but I can't *see.* I would want to
understand it all. I would want to have it exhibited, explained. That's
why the idea of purgatory is so moving."[15] The church's serious
concern about sin and penance answers such needs and helps people
to see how their living and dying are of consequence. The life reviews
that Sr. Sharon Burns and her staff initiate meet these needs among
their dying patients.

In his book *The Call of Stories,* the well-known Harvard psychi-
atrist Robert Coles tells a story that reveals how a physician attentive
to these needs in his patients is able to apply the wisdom of penance
to heal not just body and mind but spirit and soul. The story concerns
a middle-aged polio patient Coles encountered early in his medical
practice. "He had been a tough lawyer and businessman, he wanted

13. Burns, "The Spirituality of Dying," p. 50.
14. Murdoch, *Nuns and Soldiers* (New York: Viking/Penguin Books, 1981), pp.
71-72.
15. Murdoch, *Nuns and Soldiers,* p. 73.

me to know," Coles writes. "He had given little thought to others, he had paid exclusive attention to his own ambitions."[16] The man's vocal self-accusations, Job-like questioning, and incessant lamentation of his condition got on the nerves of Coles and the entire staff. They all came to view him as "a manipulative egotist" (p. 170).

Coles was troubled by his reaction to this patient. Perhaps there was something really conscientious in this man's behavior. And if that was so, what might he do as a physician to accept and respond to that sincerity and need? Coles had been reading Tolstoy while thinking about this patient. He did not see him as "a Tolstoyan figure, eager to repent and redeem himself; rather, he was the same shrewd bargainer he'd always been" (p. 168). Nevertheless, Coles's girlfriend urged him to loan the man his personal copy of Tolstoy's collected short stories, and he did so.

> When I saw him a day later, he told me he had read "The Death of Ivan Ilych." He said nothing of his reaction. I began to realize, with his silence, that I had really set him up, in my mind, for a no-win situation. If he told me effusively that he liked the story, I would have doubted his sincerity. . . . If he'd been indifferent to Tolstoy or critical of his writing — well, what else did I (so confidently!) expect, given my negative judgment of his character. (P. 172)

Later the man returned the book. As Coles walked out of the room, it occurred to him that the man hadn't really thanked him for loaning it to him. But as he flipped through the pages of the volume, "as if to reclaim them," he found a slip of paper bearing the patient's handwriting: "Dear Doctor, thanks for lending me this book. On my death bed I'll think of Ilych" (p. 172).

16. Coles, *The Call of Stories* (Boston: Houghton Mifflin, 1989), p. 168. Subsequent references to this volume will be made parenthetically in the text.

Coles wrote back, "Please know that I admire your courage as you take on the rehabilitation, and if I can be of any help, anytime, let me know. I love Tolstoy, and I love seeing you read his stories" (p. 173). Patient and physician became friends and spent much time together during the course of the patient's recovery discussing his life and Tolstoy's books. Here is one instance of a life review in which a physical cure was superseded by repentance and spiritual healing.

Suffering and Dying under the Sign of the Cross

I am now rejoicing in my suffering for your sake, and in my flesh I am completing what is lacking in Christ's afflictions for the sake of his body, that is, the church.

Colossians 1:24

The Orthodox tradition places suffering and death within the narrative and symbolic context of Christ's suffering on the cross and his resurrection. This is reflected in baptism and carried forward through all of the major Christian sacraments, including the rites of holy unction and burial. Through these rites and rituals, the Orthodox Church helps the faithful map their suffering and grief onto the suffering and death of Christ. By exploring how this happens in Christian practice, we can gain a much surer sense of the Christian understanding of what it means to live one's life toward dying.

Sr. Burns tells many stories about how she applies this practice of suffering and dying under the sign of the cross in her ministry to patients at Stella Maris Hospice. Psychologists would say that she is seeing "cognitive transformation" in her patients, but Burns believes that much more than just a *cognitive* transformation is involved: she observes events in the lives of her patients that comprehend a spiritual reality. Hope and peace replace despair and agony in a manner that she can only describe as spiritual — as a work of grace.

She tells the story of a terminally ill thirty-two-year-old mother of two married to a young college instructor. The hospital staff had done everything that they could to relieve her physical pain, but still she was tormented. Sr. Burns was asked as chaplain to talk with the young woman and find the source of her distress. She asked the woman if she could say what was bothering her. "All I can think about is my comfort, being relieved of pain," she said. "And you feel guilty about that?" asked Sr. Sharon. "Oh my God, yes," she replied. Sr. Sharon then asked the woman if she felt that she needed to "offer up" and release her pain so that it would no longer weigh down upon her. She gave the woman a choice: she could either go on cursing herself or God and die or she could hand her suffering over to Christ. Because the young wife and mother was a believing Christian, it was possible to begin a discussion about Jesus' suffering and agony on the cross. This opened up a way for the woman to "objectivize" her pain, to place it in the context of sacrifice and offering to God. As a result, a profound change came over her, and she was able to return to her home for a period of time before her death. She used this time to reach a peace within herself and with her family.

Sharon Burns's ministry to the dying includes meditation on the cross. Through baptism and chrismation, Christ is inscribed onto every Christian, and in the Eucharist Christ makes his home in our mortal flesh. His cross becomes ours, as a source not of suffering but of relief from it. Our suffering and dying become his share of his unique and redemptive suffering and death on the cross. This is what St. Paul means when he says, "I am now rejoicing in my suffering for your sake, and in my flesh I am completing what is lacking in Christ's afflictions for the sake of his body, that is, the church." Sr. Burns also counseled the young wife and mother that it might never be possible to remove all of her suffering. Even if the physical pain was eased with medicine, the suffering caused by the thought of separation from loved ones could not be wholly relieved. The young woman understood this and accepted it.

Liturgy and rite offer the sick and the dying a special voice with which to express their pain. Suffering that remains isolated in the body or in the mind affects the whole being of a person, not just the body or the mind. It threatens the normal communication and communion of body, mind, and soul. A person's entire attention might become riveted on a single organ or limb, until, as Auden puts it, "a bandage hides the place where each is living." A person can lose identity with her body or become depressed. Her body might no longer enable her to relate to the world and savor it as she once did, or her mind, which once helped her to communicate with others and lit the course of successful living, may in sickness spread the darkness of tormenting thoughts and memories over her life. Penance and forgiveness given and proffered can actually release sick or dying people from the isolation brought on by their affliction; these Christian practices can also occasion a helpful conversation between the sufferer and a compassionate listener.[17]

Salvation and Healing within the Communion of Saints

The fact that God has identified with our suffering and dying in Jesus Christ does not mean that we no longer have to face sin, suffering, or death. Suffering and death have eschatological dimensions that reach beyond our temporal lives. The Byzantine Rite of

17. For an excellent discussion of these points, see Mary Therese Lysaught, "Sharing Christ's Passion: A Critique of the Role of Suffering in the Discourse of Biomedical Ethics from the Perspective of the Theological Practice of Anointing of the Sick" (Ph.D. diss., Duke University, 1992), especially p. 282.

Holy Unction assures the sick or dying person that Christ's freely given death on the cross is a victory over mortality that makes a lie of the claims and aims of all the demonic forces that exert power over us, but Christ's sacrifice does not relieve us from dying an earthly death. Rather, because of Christ even physical death is placed within the context of a history of salvation from mortality that includes Old Testament figures, persons healed by Christ, and holy martyrs and confessors of the church who suffered or died in their obedience to Christ and in the way of the cross. The Byzantine rite recalls these biblical and postbiblical figures in the prayers and hymns that precede the act of anointing, thus joining the natural healing symbolism of oil with the biblical and sacramental meaning of anointment as the mark of salvation and a person's full incorporation into the communion of saints. This communion transcends mortality. It encompasses all of salvation history together with the second coming, the last judgment, and the final bodily resurrection of the dead.

In this special way, the Byzantine rite connects personal suffering and death and the eschatological communion of saints with God's present providential care and power over sin, sickness, and mortality. This is in keeping with the conviction of all the patristic fathers that the communion of the saints constitutes the very presence of Christ in the midst of the church, that it is the fullness of his body, the womb that gives birth to immortal life.

The recitation of the names of biblical figures, saints, and martyrs in the Byzantine rite concludes with a reading of the story of the Good Samaritan (Luke 10:25-38). This draws all of the earlier prayers that call on Christ for help and succor into a single powerful vision of God's desire that we ourselves come to the rescue of those among us who are afflicted and helpless. We are reminded that care for the sick and dying is entrusted to the church by the God into whose everlasting care all human beings are destined to be received.

Priests of Our Own Dying and Death

One last element of dying under the sign of the cross needs to be mentioned: each of us is called to be the priest of our own death. Christian baptism makes this call, and holy unction confirms it. Not just the priest but everyone present at the rite of holy unction assumes a priestly sacrificial role as sufferers and co-sufferers under the sign of the cross. The Letter to the Hebrews defends this priestly calling to suffer and die in the way of the cross, pointing to Christ as the model and fulfillment:

> In the days of his flesh, Jesus offered up prayers and supplications, with loud cries and tears, to the one who was able to save him from death, and he was heard because of his reverent submission. Although he was a Son, he learned obedience through what he suffered; and having been made perfect, he became the source of eternal salvation for all who obey him, having been designated by God a high priest according to the order of Melchizedek. (5:7-10)

A prayer of the Byzantine Rite of Holy Unction recollects baptism and in this manner connects sin, sickness, and death with salvation under the sign of the cross: "For thou art a great and marvelous God, who keepest thy covenant and thy mercy toward them that love thee; who givest remission of sin through thy Holy Child, Jesus Christ; who regeneratest us from sin by holy Baptism, and who sanctifiest us with thy Holy Spirit."[18] The same prayer, which immediately precedes anointing by oil, also invokes the cruciform symbolism of healing and incorporating persons into the royal priesthood of Christian believers:

18. *Service Book of the Holy Orthodox–Catholic Apostolic Church*, p. 344.

Inasmuch as it hath not pleased thee that we should be cleansed by blood, but by holy Oil, thou didst give unto us the image of the Cross, that we might become the flock of Christ, a royal priesthood, a holy nation; and didst purify us by water, and sanctify us by the Holy Spirit. Do thou, the same Master, O Lord, vouchsafe unto us in grace in this ministry as thou didst vouchsafe it unto Moses, thy servant, who found favor in thy sight; and unto Samuel, beloved of thee; and unto John, thy chosen one; and unto all those who, from generation to generation, have been acceptable unto thee. In like manner, make us also to be ministers of the new Covenant of thy Son upon this Oil, which thou hast acquired unto thyself through the precious blood of thy Christ; that putting away earthly lusts, we die unto sin, and live unto righteousness, being clothed upon with him through the anointing with sanctification of this Oil which we are about to summon to our aid.[19]

There are few prayers in Christian liturgy that so fully express the meaning of salvation from sin and death and are as richly descriptive of the synergy of human and divine activity through which redemptive death is accomplished. This prayer hearkens back to the etymological meaning of salvation as rescue and healing and makes it quite clear that God calls the church into being in order to be a community that cares for each of its members through sickness and death as well as through health and happiness. Fittingly, the prayer concludes with this exhortation and blessing:

Let this Oil, O Lord, become the oil of gladness, the oil of sanctification, a royal robe, an armor of might, the averting of every work of the Devil, the seal of immunity from snares, the joy of the heart, an eternal rejoicing; that they who shall be

19. *Service Book of the Holy Orthodox–Catholic Apostolic Church,* p. 344.

anointed of this Oil of regeneration may be terrible unto their adversaries, and may shine in the radiance of the Saints, having neither spot nor wrinkle; and that they may attain unto thy rest everlasting, and receive the prize of their high calling.[20]

Healing and Hope: Resurrection and Health Care

O then, weary then why should we tread?
O why are we so haggard at the heart, so care-coiled,
    care-killed, so fagged, so fashed, so cogged, so cumbered
When the thing we freely forfeit is kept with fonder care,
Fonder a care kept than we could have kept it, kept
Far with fonder care (and we, we should have lost it)
    finer, fonder
A care kept — Where kept? do but tell us where kept,
    where. —
Yonder. — What high as that! We follow,
    now we follow. — Yonder, yes yonder, yonder,
Yonder.
                  Gerard Manley Hopkins, "The Golden Echo"

The church's theology of resurrection and eternal life is, of course, an obvious resource of hope in the care of the sick and dying. But this theology, like the theology of sin and penance, is also liable to abuse. A condescending cheerfulness and insistence on Christian hope can be just as alienating and abusive as an insensitive or morbid preoccupation with sin and making amends. The strong emphasis on sin and penance in the Orthodox rites, however, precludes this cheapening of the hope in the resurrection. Christ died for the *sins*

---

20. *Service Book of the Holy Orthodox–Catholic Apostolic Church*, pp. 344-45.

of all to remove the curse of guilt and abolish death, with its sting
of emptiness and desolation. Through his dying and our participation in it, death has been transformed into a passage to eternal life.
Death that was the wages of sin becomes the end of sins. God does
not remove all the pain and anguish of living or dying — Christ
himself experienced much pain and anguish — but the resurrection
means that God reaches "even into the hollowness of nonexistence
. . . to confer life."[21] Or again, in Hopkins's turn of phrase, it
signifies that if we will be willing to "freely forfeit" the life we
cherish, it will be "kept with fonder a care,/Fonder a care kept than
we could have kept it."

This is not to suggest that the Christian doctrine of resurrection
is concerned only with personal immortality, however. Some have
characterized the universal human desire for a reunion with deceased
loved ones as immature or ignorant. But human love is too deep,
participating as it does in the agapic and mutual love of the Holy
Trinity, for this desire and yearning to be dismissed cavalierly. Mere
individual immortality does not satisfy this love. Some envision hell
as a state of individual immortality bereft of communion, as in the
Lukan story of the rich man and the beggar Lazarus (16:19-31).
The Christian hope is for resurrection and the fullness of life in
love. The whole fabric of our existence animated by love and filled
with the beings whom we have loved is what matters to us and to
God.

This is why something also needs to be said about the meaning
of Christian hope in the resurrection for the bereaved who are left
behind. As we are bound together in sin, so also in death. The
bereaved experience a double death — the death of the loved one
and their own death proleptically as they are left to go on living. I
do not know of a more moving and powerful expression in Christian

21. Jaroslav Pelikan, *The Shape of Death* (Nashville: Abingdon Press, 1961),
p. 27.

liturgy of this connection that the bereaved have with the dead and of the need that those living and left behind have for comfort and continued love than the closing prayer of the Armenian Rite of Burial of a Layperson. The central metaphor is a journey back to God in the company of all the saints. The prayer also asks God to forgive the living for their weaknesses and to give them strength to go on. It reads in part,

> Blessed art thou, Lord our God, who art the ease and quiet of the afflicted, and dost welcome the spirits that are gone to rest. Do thou accept the spirit of this thy servant unto his good. And dissipate all sorrow and mourning in those that love him, and have followed him here to dismiss him on his long and distant journey. And they are torn with grief because he is gone on a far journey and will never return, and yet more because they are separated from him for a time, while it is theirs to travel on in this crowded and tempestuous life. And do thou accept in thy good pleasure their tempered sorrow and tears, and not unto thine anger. Comfort and console their failing hearts through the advent of thy grace; and strengthen their perplexed minds by the sending of thy Holy Spirit.[22]

Each and every one of us is a sojourner through this life to the next. Some have only begun the journey; others are already near to the far side. Through it all, we must not forget that the journey is *with* others and *toward* others and that love stays our course to the blessed destination. Love and death are profoundly related throughout the journey. All earthly love is imperfect; all faith in God is incomplete. Were love perfect and faith complete, death would have no sting. It would not leave us feeling abandoned or desolate. Grief and sorrow over the deaths of loved ones are signs

22. *Rituale Armenorum*, p. 132.

of human weakness and the failure of faith. They give reason for repentance. Yet grief and sorrow are also signs that love abides in us as it did in Jesus when he wept at the grave of his friend Lazarus. And so God the Father in his infinite love condescends to forgive our weaknesses, blesses our tears, and answers our sorrow with the comfort of his Holy Spirit.

When Sr. Burns told me the story of the young wife and mother who gained comfort from reflection on the cross, she cautioned that "we must not forget about the theology of resurrection. Jesus showed us that we must overcome sickness and pain. Hospice work," she insisted, "reflects a theology of resurrection."[23] Burns counseled her patient with this theology of resurrection. "While on earth, Jesus anticipated the resurrected life — when there would be no more pain or crying or dying — by curing of the blind, the deaf, and the lame, and by his raising from the dead. Like Jesus, we must cooperate with God in overcoming pain and suffering wherever we can."[24] But Sr. Burns also reminded her patient that there is some pain — the pain of separation from loved ones — that cannot be removed by human hands. We must take the cross with us into and through death so that Christ can remove the weight of death from us once and for all.

Sr. Burns's use of the theology of resurrection in her care for the dying is a good model. It respects and insists on the strongest possible connection between the cross and the resurrection, mysteries the depth and profundity of which are indicated in the Gospels in descriptions of the marks of the nails and spear evident in the risen body of Christ. When Sr. Burns afforded the young woman the opportunity to express her deepest fear and source of sadness about the prospect that death would separate her from husband and children, this did not invite despair. Working with

23. Burns, in an interview with the author conducted in June of 1993.
24. Burns, "The Spirituality of Dying," p. 49.

the young woman's faith in the resurrection, she guided her patient to the fullest and truest understanding of what Jesus meant when he said to Martha, after bringing her brother Lazarus back to life, "I am the resurrection and the life" (John 11:25). St. John reports that many friends went to the home of Martha and Mary to console them about their brother. But Martha and Mary waited for Jesus because they believed that he could do more. They believed that he could restore their brother to health and fullness of life. The new life of resurrection includes the whole fabric of our lives restored. It means communion with God in eternity and with all the persons to whom we were bound in love during our temporal lives.

Conclusion

Throughout this book, I have been trying to cast some light on theological convictions that belong to a Christian understanding of death, euthanasia, and care for the dying. Yet I have cautioned that in our culture these convictions may not be welcome or understood. Walker Percy rightly showed that Fr. Simon Smith's position will be perceived as strange and extreme by those who have fallen prey to the thanatos syndrome.

It is no small task in our increasingly secular society to put a Christian theology of death and ethic of care for the dying into practice. But for that very reason it is all the more important for Christians to live their lives toward dying faithfully, as a witness. This culture, which was once deeply informed by biblical faith, is rapidly losing its memory of the reasons that led it to object to the casual taking of life. In this environment, Christians need to con-centrate more of their energies into the ongoing life and pedagogy of the church. The ethic I have described is church-centered. It cannot be disconnected from the community of faith in which it is learned and practiced. It cannot be reduced to a mere set of universal principles and rules that can be taught in secular medical ethics courses. It is intimately connected with the cardinal beliefs and practices of the church concerning creation and redemption. It belongs to a people who have been formed by these convictions and practices and who receive the care of the church from baptism through the whole of their lives. It is located within a broader tradition of pastoral theology and care. Caring for the sick and dying begins with caring for the healthy and living. The sacraments, Christian catechetical instruction, and preaching are the precedents and, in some real sense, the preconditions and context of this ethic. The resources that the Christian faith holds for living toward our dying in freedom and with hope and courage cannot be instantaneously transmitted to the sick person waiting for death whose flesh is already ravaged and mind tormented by disease. Nor are these resources of faith likely to be helpful to the sick and bereaved who have not been nurtured throughout their lives in that faith. The meaning for living and dying that faith provides must be owned over a lifetime.

Yet at the risk of appearing to contradict myself, I want to say that even while the primary location of this book's ethic is the church, the church's own special ministry of healing is not — indeed *must not* — be limited to believers. There are secular outlooks on medical ethics that converge with the diagnoses, prescriptions, and prognoses of the church. Those who hold these outlooks will see in limited but nonetheless significant ways the truth in the Christian ethic. And others can be persuaded. Christian medical professionals who bring their faith into their practice can make a difference for sick people who do not believe in the God of the Jewish and Christian Scriptures. I agree with William F. May's assertion that "it is angelism to assume that the sole witness of the church to the dying and the bereaved is the testimony of theology alone. A ministry to the flesh is a true and valid ministry."[25] For according to the Christian faith, that flesh is shared by all human beings. The Word assumed our common flesh and lived and died with it, just as all human beings live and die as one humanity.

And even where the church is not accepted, faith is still relevant to medicine. Christ left the church with a command to imitate and fulfill his mission of healing spirit and flesh. The church is called to convert the world through its example and service. It must serve the world not for its own sake but for the sake of all whom the Father wants as sons and daughters. Healing — deep and salvific healing — depends on faith. Christ demonstrated this in his own ministry over and over again. But he did not force faith; rather, he called it into being through his compassionate care for the flesh of the other. Medicine is a noble art, but it too needs the redemption afforded by the church's ministry.

25. May, "The Sacral Power of Death in Contemporary Experience," p. 181.

Index